GAIL BORDEN
PUBLIC LIBRARY DISTRICT
ELGIN, ILLINOIS

COMPACT *Research*

Self-Injury Disorder

Peggy J. Parks

Diseases and Disorders

ReferencePoint Press®

San Diego, CA

© 2011 ReferencePoint Press, Inc.

For more information, contact:
ReferencePoint Press, Inc.
PO Box 27779
San Diego, CA 92198
www. ReferencePointPress.com

ALL RIGHTS RESERVED.
No part of this work covered by the copyright hereon may be reproduced or used in any form or by any means—graphic, electronic, or mechanical, including photocopying, recording, taping, Web distribution, or information storage retrieval systems—without the written permission of the publisher.

Picture credits:
Cover: iStockphoto.com
Maury Asseng: 31–33, 45–47, 60–62, 74–76
Photos.com: 11
Science Photo Library: 13

LIBRARY OF CONGRESS CATALOGING-IN-PUBLICATION DATA

Parks, Peggy J., 1951–
    Self-injury disorder / by Peggy J. Parks.
        p. cm. — (Compact research series)
    Includes bibliographical references and index.
    ISBN-13: 978-1-60152-112-5 (hardback)
    ISBN-10: 1-60152-112-X (hardback)
    1. Self-mutilation—Juvenile literature. I. Title.
    RJ506.S44P28   2011
    618.92'8582—dc22
                                                                    2009050483

Contents

Foreword — 4

Self-Injury Disorder at a Glance — 6

Overview — 8

What Is Self-Injury Disorder? — 20
  Primary Source Quotes — 27
  Facts and Illustrations — 30

Why Do People Intentionally Injure Themselves? — 34
  Primary Source Quotes — 41
  Facts and Illustrations — 44

What Are the Prevention and Treatment
  Options for Self-Injurers? — 48
  Primary Source Quotes — 56
  Facts and Illustrations — 59

Can People Overcome Self-Injury Disorder? — 63
  Primary Source Quotes — 70
  Facts and Illustrations — 73

Key People and Advocacy Groups — 78

Chronology — 80

Related Organizations — 82

For Further Research — 86

Source Notes — 88

List of Illustrations — 91

Index — 92

About the Author — 96

Foreword

66Where is the knowledge we have lost in information?99

—T.S. Eliot, "The Rock."

As modern civilization continues to evolve, its ability to create, store, distribute, and access information expands exponentially. The explosion of information from all media continues to increase at a phenomenal rate. By 2020 some experts predict the worldwide information base will double every 73 days. While access to diverse sources of information and perspectives is paramount to any democratic society, information alone cannot help people gain knowledge and understanding. Information must be organized and presented clearly and succinctly in order to be understood. The challenge in the digital age becomes not the creation of information, but how best to sort, organize, enhance, and present information.

ReferencePoint Press developed the *Compact Research* series with this challenge of the information age in mind. More than any other subject area today, researching current issues can yield vast, diverse, and unqualified information that can be intimidating and overwhelming for even the most advanced and motivated researcher. The *Compact Research* series offers a compact, relevant, intelligent, and conveniently organized collection of information covering a variety of current topics ranging from illegal immigration and deforestation to diseases such as anorexia and meningitis.

The series focuses on three types of information: objective single-author narratives, opinion-based primary source quotations, and facts and statistics. The clearly written objective narratives provide context and reliable background information. Primary source quotes are carefully selected and cited, exposing the reader to differing points of view. And facts and statistics sections aid the reader in evaluating perspectives. Presenting these key types of information creates a richer, more balanced learning experience.

For better understanding and convenience, the series enhances information by organizing it into narrower topics and adding design features that make it easy for a reader to identify desired content. For example, in *Compact Research: Illegal Immigration*, a chapter covering the economic impact of illegal immigration has an objective narrative explaining the various ways the economy is impacted, a balanced section of numerous primary source quotes on the topic, followed by facts and full-color illustrations to encourage evaluation of contrasting perspectives.

The ancient Roman philosopher Lucius Annaeus Seneca wrote, "It is quality rather than quantity that matters." More than just a collection of content, the *Compact Research* series is simply committed to creating, finding, organizing, and presenting the most relevant and appropriate amount of information on a current topic in a user-friendly style that invites, intrigues, and fosters understanding.

Self-Injury Disorder at a Glance

What It Is

Health-care professionals define self-injury as the deliberate act of harming oneself that results in damage to the body, but without conscious suicidal intent.

Why People Self-Injure

The most common factor that people give for self-injury is that it gives them immediate relief from unbearable emotional pain.

Ways That People Self-Injure

The most common self-injury method is cutting with razor blades or other sharp objects. People also self-injure by burning themselves, pulling out their hair, taking poisonous substances, and/or embedding needles, staples, unfolded paper clips, and/or shards of glass under their skin.

Complications of Self-Injury

Numerous health-related risks can result from self-injuries, such as infection of cuts and abrasions, intestinal damage or death if poisons have been ingested, and/or life-threatening blood loss if major blood vessels are accidentally cut.

Suicide Risk

The act of self-injury is usually not a suicide attempt. But self-injurers have a markedly higher risk of attempting suicide compared with people who do not self-injure.

Who Self-Injures

Self-injury is most common among adolescents (both male and female), but adults have also been shown to self-injure.

Prevalence of Self-Injury

An exact number of people who self-injure is unknown. Some experts estimate that 15 to 22 percent of adolescents and young adults intentionally injure themselves at least once in their lifetimes.

Causes of Self-Injury

Some common risk factors include a history of childhood trauma (including physical, sexual, and/or emotional abuse), family environments where expression of feelings was strongly discouraged, and emotional or physical neglect during childhood.

Accompanying Disorders

People who suffer from borderline personality disorder, obsessive-compulsive disorder, or depression have a higher risk of self-injuring. The same is true of people who are autistic or who suffer from eating disorders such as anorexia or bulimia.

Prevention and Treatment

Prevention programs for this disorder are rare. People who seek treatment for self-injury often undergo intensive psychotherapy, which helps them focus on facing their traumas and other underlying reasons why they feel the need to harm themselves.

Overcoming Self-Injurious Behavior

With help many people are able to overcome the desire to injure themselves deliberately, but the relapse rate is high.

Overview

❝Somewhere I had learned that when I broke my skin, my body released the deep tension built up inside me.❞

—Brittany Burden, a young woman from Oklahoma who struggled with self-injury for seven years.

❝While self-injury may bring a momentary sense of calm and a release of tension, it's usually followed by guilt and shame and the return of painful emotions.❞

—The Mayo Clinic, a world-renowned medical practice headquartered in Rochester, Minnesota.

When Becki Bagnato was 13 years old, she accidentally broke a glass one day while cleaning her bedroom. She had been struggling with the typical emotions experienced by young teenagers, but her angst was compounded by her father's abrupt disappearance from her life and her brother's battle with drug addiction. Bagnato looked at the broken pieces and wondered, "What would it feel like if I cut my hand?"[1] She picked up a shard of glass and lightly dragged it across her palms, and then dug it in deeper until she began to bleed. There was a sharp pain followed by steady throbbing—and suddenly Bagnato felt a curious sense of calm and relief. On that day her long struggle with self-injury disorder began.

Over the following years Bagnato expanded the methods she used to injure herself. She slashed her arms, legs, and stomach with anything sharp she could get her hands on, including broken glass and razor blades. When her scars began to heal, she dug them off to reopen the wounds, and she sometimes sprayed her cuts with hair spray to intensify the pain. She also burned her body with cigarette lighters. Bagnato injured herself multiple times each day: in the morning before school, during the afternoon in the school restroom, and at home in the evening. There were many times when she woke up in the middle of the night and cut herself because it made her "forget all the crap going on in my life," and she says when she saw herself bleeding it "would give me a sense of being alive."[2]

When she was at the lowest point in her life, Bagnato says that she spent every second of the day being obsessed with the need to injure herself and even dreamed about doing it at night when she slept. "I was cutting 10-plus times a day," she says, "and still, if I didn't do it, I would feel like I was missing something."[3] Fortunately, Bagnato found the help she needed to overcome self-injury disorder. With support from her family and friends, along with years of medication, therapy, and soul searching, she was able to end the destructive cycle that threatened to ruin her life. But today, even though she has not intentionally injured herself for a couple of years, she admits that it is still a struggle for her—and may continue to be for a very long time.

> " The most common reason people give for injuring themselves is that it helps reduce severe tension and stress and gives them a sense of relief. "

What Is Self-Injury Disorder?

Sometimes called self-inflicted violence, self-abuse, or self-mutilation, self-injury disorder is defined as the act of intentionally inflicting physical harm on oneself that causes damage to the body. The most common reason people give for injuring themselves is that it helps reduce severe tension and stress and gives them a sense of relief. Even though the injuries may hurt, the physical pain offsets deep emotional pain and makes the person feel alive and in control—and after a while some people stop feeling the pain altogether. Michael Hollander, a psychologist who specializes in treating people who self-injure, counseled a 15-year-old girl named Sara who had been cutting herself since middle school. She told him that she cut herself two or three times a week, and in times of stress she did it more often. When he asked her what she meant by "stress," she described feeling emotionally overwhelmed, as though she wanted to "jump out of her skin."[4]

Most self-injurers do not have suicidal intentions when they deliberately harm themselves. In fact, their goal is quite different, as Deb Martinson from the American Self-Harm Information Clearinghouse writes: "People who inflict physical harm on themselves are often doing it in an attempt to maintain psychological integrity—it's a way to keep from killing themselves."[5] Nor is self-injury a way of seeking attention; often it is the opposite. Most people feel guilty and embarrassed and go out of their way to hide their scars so no one will see them. They do this by wearing long-sleeved shirts and long pants, even in hot weather, and covering their wrists with jewelry or other ways of concealing wounds. That is because in general, society considers the practice of self-injury to be repugnant, and people who do it often encounter shame, disgust, horror, and even contempt. This reaction is typical not only of parents, siblings, and peers, but also of many mental health and medical professionals.

> "On the Eliminate the Stigma of Mental Illness blog, one woman wrote that she had once purposely ignited a full box of matches in her enclosed fist."

Types of Self-Inflicted Injuries

Cutting is the most common type of self-injury, usually with shards of glass, razor blades, sharp knives, or even staples. Some self-injurers carve words or phrases into their skin. When Jennifer Hatz was 14 years old, she carved the word *hate* into her arm because that was the only emotion she felt at the time. People also intentionally burn themselves. On the Eliminate the Stigma of Mental Illness blog, one woman wrote that she had once purposely ignited a full box of matches in her enclosed fist. Other methods used by self-injurers include piercing the skin with needles or other pointy objects; pulling out clumps of hair; biting an arm, leg, or hand until blood is drawn; and taking poisonous substances.

Self-injurers use many different tools to inflict harm on their bodies. Knives, such as this one, razor blades, scissors, glass, needles, staples, and even paper clips are among the tools employed by self-injurers.

A girl from Canada named Cayley used most of these methods to injure herself from the time she was 10. In the years following her first cut with scissors, she cut herself with knives, razor blades, and other sharp objects. She also burned herself, pulled out her hair, punched walls until her hands were bruised and bloody, and one time even hit herself in the eye with a hammer.

Vanessa Vega, a woman who began self-injuring when she was 14, also used multiple methods of inflicting harm on her body. She says that when she was at her lowest point and finally got up the courage to seek therapy, she was cutting herself four times a day—but her injurious behavior went far beyond cutting. She writes: "I had tried, unsuccessfully, to break my own arms and femurs, although I *had* succeeded in breaking fingers and toes, and most recently, in rupturing the protective casing around my ulna and radius bones in my right arm. Repeated blunt trauma to my right wrist and forearm left me with temporary numbness in my fingers."[6]

Complications of Self-Injury Disorder

The most obvious physical remnant of self-injury disorder is permanent scarring on the body, which may range from mild to severe. But a number of health-related problems can result from self-injuries, including serious infection of cuts and abrasions, as well as sickness, intestinal damage, or death from ingesting poisons. If a major blood vessel or artery is inadvertently cut during self-injury, this can result in life-threatening blood loss. And people who have damaged their bones and muscles run the risk of suffering from numbness and/or chronic pain.

Although the act of self-injury is not usually a suicide attempt, suicide is one of the greatest risks for those who suffer from this disorder. Feelings of helplessness, shame, and guilt can become so intense and overwhelming that the person may be driven to suicide. Clinical psychologist Wendy Lader states that people who intentionally injure themselves are nine times more likely to attempt suicide than non-self-injurers. According to Hollander, research has produced some theories about the connection between self-injury disorder and suicide attempts. One is that the longer someone continues to self-harm deliberately, the more likely he or she will be to attempt suicide. Also, many people who intentionally injure themselves report that they feel no pain in doing so, which makes them more likely than those who do feel pain to try to commit suicide.

From All Walks of Life

Self-injury disorder does not discriminate. Once believed to be an affliction that was limited to females, as many as 40 percent of those who self-injure are males. People of all races, religions, education levels, socioeconomic status, and sexual orientations deliberately harm themselves. The age range of those who self-injure also varies, but it is most common among adolescents. As the Mayo Clinic explains: "Self-injury often starts in the early teen years, when emotions are more volatile and children face increasing peer pressure, loneliness and conflicts with parents or other authority figures."[7]

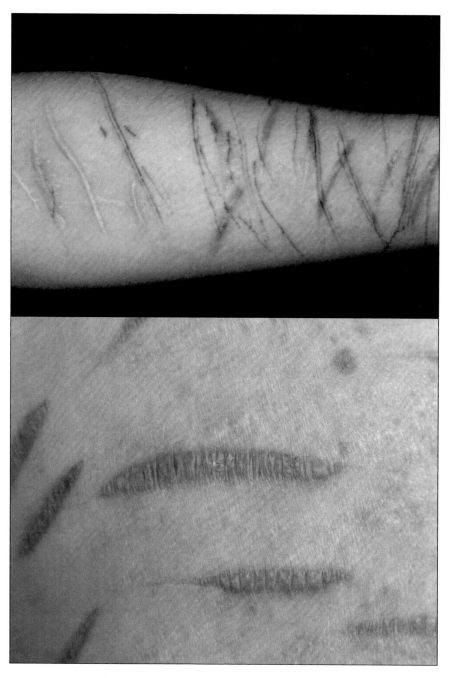

Cutting is one of the most common forms of self-injury. Raw, red lacerations provide a painful close-up view of the damage caused by a self-injurer (top). Even after the injuries heal, scarring creates a lasting reminder of the disorder (bottom).

Yet self-injurious behavior is by no means limited to teenagers. Adults deliberately harm themselves as well. One professional woman in her thirties who holds a master's degree in social work describes her 17-year struggle on a self-injury blog: "I cut myself with razors because the pain in my chest is unbearable. Almost anything can set me off. Most of all, the desire to injure myself comes when I feel like I have failed at something or when I feel someone close to me is going to leave me. . . . Cutting relieves the pain that nothing else can take away."[8] Older adults also intentionally injure themselves. Michelle Seliner, a therapist who specializes in self-injury disorder, says that the oldest patient at the Chicago treatment center where she works was 77 years old.

Prevalence of Self-Injury Disorder

It is virtually impossible to know how many people intentionally self-injure. This is largely because many are ashamed about what they do to their bodies, so they keep their self-injury a secret from their families and friends. Also, no widespread government or scientific statistics have ever been compiled, and research on self-injury disorder is sparse. One psychologist who researched the issue is Janis Whitlock, who is director of Cornell University's Self-Injurious Behavior in Adolescents and Young Adults research program. Whitlock conducted a survey among college students and found that about 17 percent, including 20 percent of women and 14 percent of men, have cut, burned, carved, or injured themselves in other ways at some point in their lives. The editors of the *Journal of Consulting and Clinical Psychology* state that self-injury is "remarkably prevalent and woefully understudied."[9]

Experts say that many people who self-injure have grown up in families where expressions of emotion and anger were not tolerated, so they never learned how to release their feelings in a healthy way.

Hollander and his colleagues believe that the incidence of self-injury disorder is on the rise, although he admits that there is no way to know for sure. One reason for the uncertainty is that self-injury is often mistakenly documented as a suicide attempt. Also, the methods researchers use to define self-injury vary widely, and there are no definite, consistent criteria for categorizing the disorder. "Consequently," Hollander writes, "the percentages given for adolescents in the general population who self-injure range from 9 to 39%; for adolescents who are hospitalized for psychiatric reasons, the range is 40 to 60%."[10] He adds that another reason the prevalence of self-injury disorder is difficult to gauge is that people are more open about it now than in the past. Even though those who self-injure are often secretive

> **One factor that makes the diagnosis especially difficult is that people who self-injure often go out of their way to hide it from family and friends.**

about it, awareness of the disorder has grown over the years. Since young people are now more apt to disclose their self-injurious behavior, at least to friends, that, too, could influence statistics about whether the disorder's prevalence is increasing.

Why Do People Intentionally Injure Themselves?

There is no clear-cut answer to the question of what causes people to deliberately harm themselves. As the Mayo Clinic states:

> The mix of emotions that triggers self-injury is complex. In general, self-injury is usually the result of an inability to cope in healthy ways with deep psychological pain. For instance, you may have a hard time regulating, expressing or understanding your emotions. Physical injury distracts you from these painful emotions or helps you feel a sense of control over an otherwise uncontrollable situation.[11]

Experts say that many people who self-injure have grown up in families where expressions of emotion and anger were not tolerated, so they never learned how to release their feelings in a healthy way. By injuring themselves, they are able to release those feelings. Those who have experienced verbal, psychological, or sexual abuse may also turn to self-injury as a way of releasing hurt, fear, and anger. In many cases self-injury disorder is thought to be associated with psychological afflictions such as depression or borderline personality disorder.

Connection with Eating Disorders

Psychologists have found that there is a close tie between self-injury and eating disorders such as anorexia nervosa and bulimia. Sharon Farber, a psychologist who specializes in self-injury, extensively researched this connection and found many commonalities between the disorders. She describes them as "an individual's attempt to solve emotional problems, to make himself or herself feel better. . . . I found that the self-injurious behavior and the bulimic behavior, especially the purging (which is the most painful part of that experience), were being used as an attempt to release tension or to interrupt or end a feeling of depression or extreme anxiety."[12]

Lauren Simmons (not her real name) personally witnessed the physical harm that someone with an eating disorder had inflicted on herself. Years ago she worked for a therapist who treated people with anorexia and bulimia, and one female patient cut herself on a regular basis. Simmons had never seen the woman's scars because she always wore long, loose-fitting pants and long-sleeved shirts, as self-injurers typically do. She describes her shocked reaction when the woman came in for therapy on a warm summer day wearing shorts and a tank top: "Her arms and legs were covered with ugly, jagged scars. They were everywhere, as though she had been brutally slashed over and over again with a razor-sharp knife. In my entire lifetime, I had never seen anything so horrid."[13] The therapist explained that the patient was not cutting in an attempt to commit suicide. Rather, she was filled with self-loathing and could not stop punishing herself.

Self-Injury Disorder and Autism

People who suffer from a complex brain disorder known as autism have a markedly high rate of self-injury. A study published in 2008 showed that autistic children were 762 percent more likely to be treated for self-inflicted injuries compared with children who did not have autism. Harold Doherty, a man from New Brunswick, Canada, says that his autistic son often engages in self-injurious behavior. He writes: "Conor came home from a great day at school. He sat at a computer as he often does to view some of his favorite sites which he has bookmarked. For some reason, slow loading pages perhaps, I am not sure, Conor became very frustrated with the computer, suffered a meltdown and began biting his hand."[14]

According to psychologist Travis Thompson, self-biting is one of the most common ways that autistic children harm themselves, and self-injury is the most difficult challenge parents of autistic children face. He says that the behavior is usually triggered by some sort of environmental event, such as an unexpected change in routine, asking the child to do something that he or she is unable to do, or the child's being in an alarming situation. These are

> " A treatment program is tailored to a patient's individual needs and usually involves intensive therapy sessions. During these sessions the person learns how to manage the underlying issues that trigger self-injury, as well as how to express anger, frustration, and stress in a healthier manner. "

particularly challenging for autistic children because they typically have poor communication skills. Thus, they may self-injure as a way of expressing frustration.

Diagnosing Self-Injury Disorder

There is no specific diagnostic test for self-injury disorder, and mental health professionals often disagree about whether it is a diagnosis in and of itself or a symptom of another psychological disorder. One factor that makes the diagnosis especially difficult is that people who self-injure often go out of their way to hide it from family and friends. So, even if they have visible scars, if they are not willing to admit that they injure themselves, all health-care professionals can do is speculate.

During mental and physical evaluations, questions are typically asked about when the self-injury began, how often the patient engages in it, what methods of self-injury are used, what emotional issues he or she faces, and what seems to trigger the self-injuring behavior. A mental health professional will also likely evaluate the person for mental illnesses that may accompany self-injury, such as depression or personality disorders.

What Are the Prevention and Treatment Options for Self-Injurers?

The Mayo Clinic states that there is no sure way to prevent self-injury. "Prevention strategies may need to involve both individuals and communities, including parents, schools, medical professionals and coaches, for instance."[15] Self-injury prevention programs are relatively uncommon, although this may begin to change as awareness grows about the seriousness of the disorder. A Chicago treatment center known as Self Abuse Finally Ends (S.A.F.E.) Alternatives has created educational materials that are available to schools that are interested in starting prevention programs. Professionals from S.A.F.E. Alternatives also conduct presentations for educators so they can learn to spot warning signs in students who might be engaging in self-injurious behavior.

As for treatment, none exists specifically for self-injury disorder. A treatment program is tailored to a patient's individual needs and usually involves intensive therapy sessions. During these sessions the person learns how to manage the underlying issues that trigger self-injury, as well as how to express anger, frustration, and stress in a healthier manner. Nor are there any medications that specifically treat self-injury disorder, although medications are sometimes prescribed to treat accompanying psychological conditions such as depression and anxiety.

Can People Overcome Self-Injury Disorder?

People can and do recover from self-injury disorder, but only if they deeply want to stop injuring themselves and are willing to work hard to accomplish that. For Tara Prutsman, who cut herself from the time she was 15, the answer was S.A.F.E. Alternatives. Prutsman had tried to stop but felt as though the behavior was out of her control, and she always relapsed. "Then last year, I went on a binge," she says, "cutting myself a few times a day. I had been very depressed, and when I told my friend how bad my condition had become, she took me to the hospital."[16] While she was there Prutsman heard about the S.A.F.E. program and decided to sign up for it. After spending two weeks as an inpatient and two weeks as an outpatient, she was able to work through her emotional trauma and get her self-abusive behavior under control. She writes: "It's constant therapy and hard work, but it's worth it. I finished this past June, and I haven't hurt myself since. . . . So many self-injurers suffer alone because they're afraid to reveal their problem. I want people to know they can get help."[17]

What Is Self-Injury Disorder?

66Self injury is any deliberate, non suicidal behaviour that inflicts physical harm on your body and is aimed at relieving emotional distress. Physical pain is often easier to deal with than emotional pain, because it causes 'real' feelings.99

—LifeSIGNS, an organization based in the United Kingdom that supports people who are affected by self-injury disorder.

66Many people who self-injure keep it a secret because they feel like they are crazy, insane and evil. They fear if they tell anyone, they might be locked away forever.99

—Colleen Thompson, editor of the Mirror-Mirror Web site for people with eating disorders.

Michael Hollander has been a psychologist for more than 30 years, and in that time he has counseled hundreds of patients who engage in self-injurious behavior. He had his first encounter with self-injury disorder when he was in his first year of postdoctoral training. Hollander was at a hospital/school for troubled youth and overheard a conversation between two young girls. At first he thought they must be fooling around because they were talking about the benefits of self-injury. He writes: "Speaking with a kind of secret excitement, they told of how burning themselves actually made them feel better and more alive. As I spoke with supervisors and colleagues, my eyes were opened to this phenomenon, and I realized that the girls had indeed been serious."[18]

After that experience Hollander decided that he wanted to focus on working with young people who intentionally harmed themselves. Throughout the years much of the knowledge he has gained has come from what he has learned from counseling them. He stresses that there are two common reasons why people self-injure: "to control the extremely painful and frightening experience of overwhelming emotions," and/or "to escape from an awful feeling of being numb and empty."[19]

A Desperate Way of Coping

Those who have extensive experience with patients who self-injure share Hollander's perspective about why people deliberately harm their bodies: that they are using it as a coping mechanism. Yet self-injury is still widely misunderstood, including by a large number of health-care professionals. According to Deb Martinson, when people encounter someone who has engaged in deliberate self-injury, their reaction is often extremely negative and not at all supportive. She writes: "In emergency rooms, people with self-inflicted wounds are often told directly and indirectly, that they are not as deserving of care as someone who has an accidental injury. They are treated badly by the same doctors who would not hesitate to do everything possible to preserve the life of an overweight, sedentary heart-attack patient."[20]

Connie Hanagan had an experience with this when she was 17 years old. She was a patient at a Massachusetts state hospital, and one day she intentionally cut her leg in three places with a piece of glass. As a way of teaching her a lesson, the doctor who stitched her wounds did not use an anesthetic. Then he told her: "Maybe you will think twice before you cut yourself again."[21] Other people who self-injure have reported having similar experiences with physicians who were unsympathetic toward them.

> **People who would never dream of deliberately harming themselves cannot possibly fathom why *anyone* would do it.**

As mystifying as self-injury disorder is to many health-care professionals, it is even more so to parents, siblings, and peers of anyone who self-injures. People who would never dream of deliberately harming themselves cannot possibly fathom why *anyone* would do it. For those who self-injure, however, it is the only way they know how to cope when emotions seem too overpowering to bear. These people may look nothing alike, come from diverse backgrounds, and be in different places in their lives, but most share one thing in common: the inability to deal with crushing pressure, feelings of helplessness, and unbearable stress. Sharon Farber explains: "For many people it's a form of their body's speaking for them. In other words, the body says for the person what they cannot allow themselves to say or know in words. It's about speaking about emotional pain that they cannot put into words, so their body speaks for them. If you want to think of the bleeding as a form of tears that they couldn't cry, I think that's a good metaphor."[22]

Brittany Burden can personally relate to deep emotional pain that drives someone to self-injure. She began injuring herself at the age of 14, when she was having trouble adjusting to a new school. One day she was at her aunt's house and found a rusty letter opener in a desk drawer. She grabbed it and began scratching herself—and that was just the beginning. By the time she was 18, she was regularly cutting herself as well as hitting herself almost daily. Burden says that at the age of 21, "round two"[23] of her real pain began.

On the outside, Burden appeared to be fine. Her college classes were going well, she had great friends, and she was close to her family—but on the inside she was hurting, and she found herself sinking deeper into depression. One day she took a pushpin off a bulletin board in an academic hall. She writes: "My heart pulsated rapidly as I dug the sharp point into my skin. On my biceps, I drew a deep vertical line. In time, after every cut I would make a new cut next to my first one across my arm, one for each time I've cut myself." Burden constantly told herself that each cut would be her last, but she found that she could not stop: "Soon, I was at my skin so many times a day that I can no longer remember the total number of cuts I made."[24]

Hearing Voices

Many people who intentionally harm themselves feel as though the decision to do so is out of their control. Some report hearing voices in their heads that order them to self-injure. This was true with one of Hollander's patients, and to her the voices were very real. Hollander calls these "auditory hallucinations" and says they are often due to underlying mental illnesses such as bipolar disorder or schizophrenia. He writes: "Frequently the 'voices' are of a harsh and critical nature and demand that the children injure themselves as punishment. The child's brain processes these 'voices' the same way it would process anything else he or she were to hear, and it can be very frightening."[25] Hollander adds that the voices seem so real to self-injurers that they feel they have no choice but to comply with their demands.

Whether they hear voices or not, many people who self-injure do so as a way of punishing themselves. This is either because they do not like the person they see in the mirror or do not feel they can live up to their own expectations and/or what others expect of them. Vanessa Vega was plagued by a voice in her head that constantly berated her, saying that she deserved to be punished. It told her that she was a lousy wife, a mediocre teacher, and too fat to model anymore. "Face it," the voice said. "Nobody cares. You're a freak! . . . You have nothing to offer. Give up. Give in. Stop jerking around and do this! Do what you know the best. Hurt."[26]

> " Many people who intentionally harm themselves feel as though the decision to do so is out of their control. "

Whenever Vega heard the voice, she felt darkness sweeping over her, rendering her helpless at fighting it off. She writes: "The darkness started coming for me on Monday. Much like the flu, it hit the base of my spine first. The slight but undeniable tingling that just won't go away. I have a chill to my bones that I cannot seem to shake, even though I take two to three hot baths a day to try and alleviate it."[27] Unable to resist the overwhelming urge to cut herself, she describes the moments that always led up to it:

> It's time.
>
> I look at my wrist and see the scars that I've put there over the last twenty years. I cry. I am living a lie. When I made my first cuts, I swore to myself they would be the last. That if I could just get over the hump, the need for scissors and razor blades and knives would be over. One day, I told myself, I would be in a better place.

Yeah, right. . . .

I take the scissors in my left hand and hold my right arm stiff. The darkness surrounds me and I let it carry me away.[28]

Embedding Objects Under the Skin

On December 3, 2008, at an annual meeting of North American radiologists, William Shiels, the chief of radiology at Nationwide Children's Hospital in Columbus, Ohio, discussed what he calls the "next phase" of self-injury: a method known as embedding. The practice involves pushing objects such as needles, staples, pencil lead, paper clips, chunks of metal or plastic, pieces of glass, safety pins, and other sharp objects under the skin of the arms, neck, feet, hands, and ankles. Shiels told of one girl who came in with a bobby pin embedded in her forearm, as well as three staples, chunks of pencil lead, glass shards, and pieces of wood. Another patient had unfolded two large paper clips and inserted one into each of her biceps.

Shiels is convinced that the practice is increasing, because he is seeing more patients who have self-injured by embedding. He explains: "We've been treating patients with accidental foreign bodies under their skin for 13 years, but before 2005, we never saw [self-inflicted] cases like this in adolescence. We believe this is out there more than people think—it's just that we didn't know what to call it or understand its significance."[29] Shiels adds that embedding is different from other types of self-injury because it is taking the behavior to the extreme. Often, people who self-injure by embedding have found that cutting no longer works for them. One of his greatest concerns is that the practice often leads to serious health complications: "They come in with pain, infections, and sometimes guilt. The infections can be very severe—putting nerves, veins, even tendons at risk."[30]

> **Known as suspension, it involves people hanging by metal hooks that have been embedded in their flesh.**

"Passive" Self-Injury

Not everyone who engages in self-injurious behavior causes their own injuries. Instead, some people prefer that others inflict the injuries on them. One example, according to Farber, is people who become obsessed with multiple body piercings and tattoos. Farber refers to this as a "passive" form of self-injury, as she explains: "With people who get themselves tattooed constantly, many of them do it not only for the way it looks but for the experience of the pain. Some people will get a buzz from the tattooing. Some people even experience this erotically and get turned on by it."

Farber adds that she is not referring to someone who gets tattooed to look cool or because his or her friends are doing it. "I am talking about people who feel a 'need' to do this to their bodies and have this kind of a physical experience. What it does for them is what cutting or burning does for others. It distracts them from the pain that is inside, the internal pain."[31]

> **Even if they desperately want to stop harming themselves, they find that impossible to do because giving up their only coping mechanism is terrifying.**

Wendy Lader points out a different form of self-injury whereby others cause the pain. Known as suspension, it involves people hanging by metal hooks that have been embedded in their flesh. Some who do it say that it helps them achieve a sense of inner peace and euphoria that comes from being able to float. Others say they suspend because the feelings they experience are more intense than they get from having their bodies repeatedly tattooed. To prepare for suspension, participants lie down on a massage table to have the hooks put in. For one performance at a nightclub in Chicago, a suspender named Amourena Tsokatos had 8 large hooks inserted: 2 in her upper back, 2 in the back of her thighs, and 2 above and below her buttocks. Ropes attached to a steel frame were woven through the hooks and then she was lifted into the air, where she floated for about 20 minutes as blood trickled down her legs.

Suspension is a highly controversial practice. Health-care experts warn that it can result in severe skin tears and infections, as dermatologist Anne

Laumann explains: "If you put metal hooks through the skin, you are making tunnels for infection."[32] Mental health professionals who specialize in self-injury say that those who participate in suspension are resorting to an extreme form of self-injury in an effort to mask emotional issues.

A Difficult Cycle to Break

People who deliberately self-injure often struggle with emotions that seem too powerful to handle. For many, this is the only way they feel equipped to deal with the pressures and stresses of daily life. Even if they desperately want to stop harming themselves, they find that impossible to do because giving up their only coping mechanism is terrifying. As one of Hollander's patients explains: "In some ways it's like an old friend who is a bit troublesome but who is always there when you need her."[33]

What Is Self-Injury Disorder?

"I have seen that nothing causes parents as much anguish as kids who deliberately cut, scratch, burn, or hurt themselves in some other fashion."

—Michael Hollander, *Helping Teens Who Cut.* New York: Guilford, 2008.

Hollander is a psychologist and an expert in the treatment of self-injury disorder.

....

"Self-inflicted injury in adolescence indicates significant emotional and psychological suffering."

—Sheila E. Crowell et al., "Parent-Child Interactions, Peripheral Serotonin, and Self-Inflicted Injury in Adolescents," *Journal of Consulting and Clinical Psychology*, no. 1, 2008. http://tbeauchaine.psych.washington.edu.

Crowell is with the Department of Psychology at the University of Washington.

....

* Editor's Note: While the definition of a primary source can be narrowly or broadly defined, for the purposes of Compact Research, a primary source consists of: 1) results of original research presented by an organization or researcher; 2) eyewitness accounts of events, personal experience, or work experience; 3) first-person editorials offering pundits' opinions; 4) government officials presenting political plans and/or policies; 5) representatives of organizations presenting testimony or policy.

> **66** Self-injury is the act of deliberately harming your own body. . . . It's not meant as a suicide attempt and isn't part of a socially acceptable cultural or artistic expression or ritual, such as tattooing. **99**

—The Mayo Clinic, "Self-Injury/Cutting," August 2, 2008. www.mayoclinic.com.

The Mayo Clinic is a world-renowned medical facility headquartered in Rochester, Minnesota.

> **66** Self-harm affects thousands of depressed teenagers each year. **99**

—Myrna M. Weissman, "Teenaged, Depressed, and Treatment Resistant: What Predicts Self-Harm?" *American Journal of Psychiatry*, April 2009. http://ajp.psychiatryonline.org.

Weissman is professor of epidemiology in psychology at Columbia University College of Physicians and Surgeons.

> **66** There are some people who do not have the intention to end their lives but they like to flirt with the idea of going a little further and die in the process. **99**

—Sharon Farber, interviewed by David Roberts, "Getting Help for Self-Harm," HealthyPlace, April 11, 2007. www.healthyplace.com.

Farber is a therapist who specializes in self-injury disorder and is the author of *When the Body Is the Target: Self-Harm, Pain and Traumatic Attachments*.

> **66** Cutting behaviors are intentional acts, often using knives and/or razor blades to slice the skin. Common locations for cutting include the wrists and ankles. **99**

—Tracy L. Cross, "Social/Emotional Needs," *Gifted Child Today*, Summer 2007.

Cross is a psychologist from Muncie, Indiana.

---

66 **Although self-harm is rarely a suicidal act, it must be taken seriously because accidental deaths do occur.** 99

—Deborah Cutter, Jaelline Jaffe, and Jeanne Segal, "Cutting and Self-Injury," HelpGuide, February 2008. http://helpguide.org.

Cutter, Jaffe, and Segal are all psychotherapists.

66 **It is only in the past several years that awareness has increased about the prevalence of SIV [self-inflicted violence] in the lives of boys and men and people from very diverse backgrounds. SIV is not a new phenomenon.** 99

—Ruta Mazelis, "Living with and Healing from Self-Injury (Self-Inflicted Violence)," Sidran Institute, January 22, 2008. http://download.ncadi.samhsa.gov.

Mazelis is a content specialist for Sidran Traumatic Stress Institute on self-harming behaviors and related issues and is the creator of the Healing Self-Injury blog and the *Cutting Edge* newsletter.

66 **Most who engage in self-injury act alone rather than in groups. They also attempt to hide their behavior.** 99

—Amal Chakraburtty, "Mental Health and Self-Injury," WebMD, March 9, 2009. www.webmd.com.

Chakraburtty is a psychiatrist in Oklahoma.

What Is Self-Injury Disorder?

- According to the organization Truth Hurts, rates of self-injury have increased in the United Kingdom over the past decade and are highest among young people, with an estimated **25,000 11- to 25-year-olds** admitted to the hospital each year with self-inflicted injuries.

- A 2007 survey among high school students in Massachusetts revealed that **17 percent** of them had engaged in self-injurious behavior at some point in their lives.

- A study published in the January 29, 2008, issue of the *Canadian Medical Association Journal* stated that nearly **17 percent** of teenagers have self-injured at least once; of these teens, **77 percent** were girls and **23 percent** were boys.

- According to a December 2008 *Newsweek* article, studies have shown that **75 percent** of people who self-injure use multiple ways of harming themselves.

- A survey of 1,000 self-injurers by the United Kingdom health charity SANE revealed that **10 percent** of respondents were male, and some did not start self-injuring until they reached midlife.

- A study in the February 2008 issue of *Journal of Consulting and Clinical Psychology* stated that of 94 girls aged 10 to 14, **56 percent** had harmed themselves at least once.

Self-Injury and Gender

Self-injurious behavior is complex and often misunderstood, even by many mental health professionals. One perception is that only females are affected by it, but studies have shown that males self-injure as well. In a survey that was published in the January 29, 2008, issue of the *Canadian Medical Association Journal*, 568 participants aged 14 to 21 were asked whether they had ever intentionally harmed themselves, and 96 said that they had. This chart shows the gender breakdown.

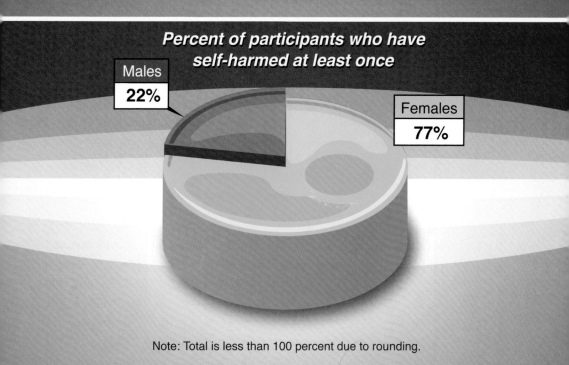

Percent of participants who have self-harmed at least once

Males
22%

Females
77%

Note: Total is less than 100 percent due to rounding.

Source: Mary K. Nixon, Paula Clotier, and S. Mikael Jannson, "Nonsuicidal Self-Harm in Youth: A Population-Based Survey," *Canadian Medical Association Journal*, January 29, 2008. www.cmaj.com.

- A study published in 2006 by researchers at Cornell University found that **one out of five** college students had cut, burned, or injured themselves in other ways at some point in their lives.

Self-Injurious Behavior Among College Students

In an effort to better understand the prevalence and nature of self-injury among those who are attending college, psychologists from Cornell University performed a comprehensive study that was published in 2006. Nearly 500 participants reported having deliberately harmed themselves at some point in their lives. These charts show their lifetime frequency of self-injury and the age when they first began.

Lifetime frequency of self-injury

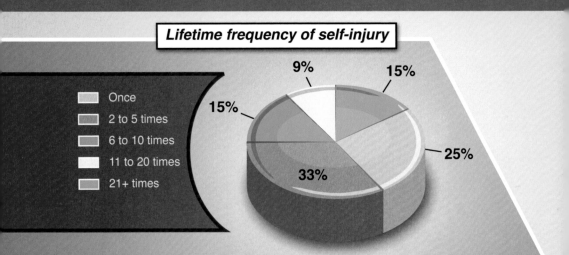

Once
2 to 5 times
6 to 10 times
11 to 20 times
21+ times

9%
15%
15%
25%
33%

Note: Total is less than 100 percent due to rounding.

Age at onset of self-injury

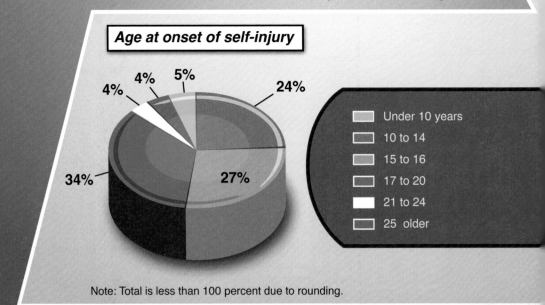

4%
4%
5%
24%
34%
27%

Under 10 years
10 to 14
15 to 16
17 to 20
21 to 24
25 older

Note: Total is less than 100 percent due to rounding.

Source: Janis Whitlock, John Eckenrode, and Daniel Silverman, "Self-Injurious Behavior in a College Population," *Pediatrics*, June 2006. http://pediatrics.aappublications.org.

Why and How People Harm Themselves

In an effort to learn more about why young people deliberately harm themselves, as well as the methods they use to do so, researchers in the United Kingdom surveyed adolescents aged 11 to 19. These graphs show some of their findings.

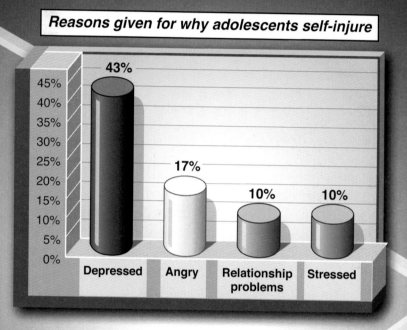

Reasons given for why adolescents self-injure

- Depressed: 43%
- Angry: 17%
- Relationship problems: 10%
- Stressed: 10%

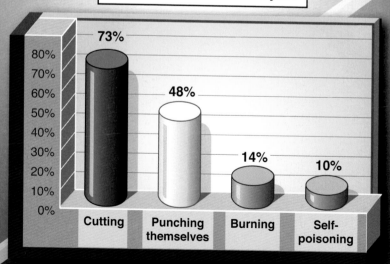

Methods used to self-injure

- Cutting: 73%
- Punching themselves: 48%
- Burning: 14%
- Self-poisoning: 10%

Source: Cheadle Royal Hospital Affinity Healthcare, "New Survey Reveals Almost One in Three Young Females Have Tried to Self-Harm," April 25, 2008, www.affinityhealth.co.uk.

Why Do People Intentionally Injure Themselves?

> 66An inability to cry, scream or yell may lead to self-injury as a way to express emotional pain. Additional reasons for self-injury may include loneliness, alienation and self-loathing.99
>
> —Steven A. King, a psychiatrist and clinical professor at the New York University School of Medicine.

> 66We wear the guise of healthy, adjusted people, but inside we are as broken as the shards of glass we cut ourselves with.99
>
> —Brittany Burden, a young woman from Oklahoma who has recovered from self-injury disorder after cutting herself for seven years.

Caitlin's parents were distraught and at an absolute loss over what to do for their daughter. She had been cutting herself several times a week for more than a year, and continued to do so even though they tried everything possible to help her. She had taken a variety of prescription medications, undergone individual therapy with a counselor, and also attended family counseling with her parents. Thinking that a change might be good for her, Caitlin's parents sent her to a different school. They tried grounding her and even locked up all the sharp objects in the house—but nothing worked. During one family counseling session, Caitlin's mother spoke of their frustration: "She's such a good kid. I know she's unhappy. I just wish that she and her therapist could find the reason for her cutting. What does it mean to her? I think if she knew why she did it, she'd be able to stop."[34]

Like Caitlin, many who deliberately harm themselves do not know why they do it. Moreover, mental health professionals have not been able to identify a specific cause—and whether self-injury is even a disorder at all is controversial. For instance, the American Psychiatric Association does not recognize self-injurious behavior as a disorder in its *Diagnostic and Statistical Manual (DSM)*. Instead, the manual only references self-injury once, as a symptom of borderline personality disorder (BPD), which is a disorder that affects how people control their emotions. Bessel van der Kolk, who is medical director of the Trauma Center in Boston and an advisor for the *DSM*, shares his opinion: "Self injury is part of a larger picture; it should never be seen as an isolated thing."[35]

> Many psychologists have concluded that a troubled childhood is the most consistent trait among those who engage in self-injurious behavior.

Even in the absence of an exact cause, those who specialize in treating patients who self-injure tend to agree that people who deliberately harm themselves share one thing in common: They are desperately seeking a release from emotional pain. As Deb Martinson writes: "In other words, they feel a strong uncomfortable emotion, don't know how to handle it (indeed, often do not have a name for it), and know that hurting themselves will reduce the emotional discomfort extremely quickly. They may still feel bad (or not), but they don't have that panicky jittery trapped feeling; it's a calm bad feeling."[36]

Childhood Trauma

Many psychologists have concluded that a troubled childhood is the most consistent trait among those who engage in self-injurious behavior. According to Sharon Farber, this usually results from a child suffering some sort of trauma during his or her formative years. Although this may result from physical, psychological, or sexual abuse, or physi-

> **Even though a history of abuse is common among those who self-injure, not everyone who self-injures has been abused, nor do all people who have experienced abuse engage in self-injurious behavior.**

cal or emotional neglect, these factors do not always play a role in whether someone self-injures. Farber explains: "People experience events very, very differently. Trauma can be parents splitting up and all of a sudden the child no longer sees his or her father or mother, and that is a terrible trauma for a child, and that is terribly painful. . . . Trauma comes in many different forms."[37]

Yet many therapists who have worked with people who self-injure have learned that their patients did experience abuse during childhood. Often, abused children blame themselves and are filled with self-hatred, erroneously believing that they somehow deserved the abusive treatment. Those who self-injure may use it as a way of coping with deep feelings of hurt, anger, and fear—feelings that they have kept buried because they were not allowed to express them. Martinson explains:

> They learned that certain feelings weren't allowed. In abusive homes, they may have been severely punished for expressing certain thoughts and feelings. At the same time, they had no good role models for coping. You can't learn to cope effectively with distress unless you grow up around people who are coping effectively with distress. How could you learn to cook if you'd never seen anyone work in a kitchen?[38]

Tara Prutsman attributes her battle with self-injury to her troubled childhood. When she was growing up, her mother suffered from chronic illness. Much of her father's time was spent caring for his wife, so he left Tara's care to her two older brothers. Tara says that their "idea of parenting was to abuse me verbally and physically." She explains the effect this had on her: "Since nobody talked about feelings in my family (I'd even get yelled at for crying), cutting myself was a way for me to release my emotions."[39] At first she scratched her arms with safety pins, but she soon began slicing her skin with razor blades several times a week. When she could no longer hide the scars on her arms, she started cutting her thighs. "The depth of the wounds would vary," she writes, "depending on my level of stress. The worst I felt, the deeper I cut."[40]

Several studies have confirmed the link between physical and/or sexual abuse during childhood and self-injury disorder, such as one that was published in April 2007. Researchers from Harvard University and Boston University School of Medicine analyzed 86 adolescents, including 69 females and 17 males. The participants were asked questions about their childhoods, such as whether they had ever been diagnosed with depression and if they had engaged in self-injurious behavior in the past 12 months. Upon completion of the study, the researchers concluded that the strongest factors in whether the young people self-injured were sexual abuse and emotional neglect during the formative years. Referring to the behavior as NSSI (non-suicidal self-injury), they write:

> People who experience maltreatment during childhood in the form of repeated insults, excessive criticism, or some form of physical abuse may come to adopt a similarly critical view of themselves over time through modeling the behavior of those who criticized and abused them. This . . . may ultimately manifest in the engagement in NSSI as an extreme form of self-punishment or self-abuse whenever they disapprove of their own behavior.[41]

Biological Factors

Even though a history of abuse is common among those who self-injure, not everyone who self-injures has been abused, nor do all people who have experienced abuse engage in self-injurious behavior. This causes health-care professionals to wonder if biological factors might be involved. It is much the same as someone whose family has a history of clinical depression and, as a result, has a significantly higher likelihood of developing it. According to the Mayo Clinic, evidence has suggested that people who have a family history of self-injury, suicide, or other self-destructive acts are more prone to harming themselves intentionally. Wendy Lader states that no gene has been specifically tied to self-injury, but she says "there may be some predisposition for lower tolerance for frustration."[42]

Several studies have shown that people with self-injury disorder have an imbalance of serotonin, a chemical in the brain that serves as a regulator of emotions, appetite, and sleep. Serotonin is a neurotransmitter, meaning that it is used by nerve cells (known as neurons) as they constantly send messages to one another. If there is a disruption in serotonin levels, this can interrupt the brain's normal function and behavior. Martinson explains how this could potentially affect someone's tendency toward self-injury:

> Just as it's suspected that the way the brain uses serotonin may play a role in depression, so scientists think that problems in the serotonin system may predispose some people to self-injury by making them tend to be more aggressive and impulsive than most people. This tendency toward impulsive aggression, combined with a belief that their feelings are bad or wrong, can lead to the aggression being turned on the self.[43]

The connection between serotonin levels and self-injury was the subject of a study published in 2008 in the *Journal of Consulting and Clinical Psychology*. The researchers examined 21 adolescents who did not engage in self-injurious behavior and 20 who did. They found that serotonin imbalances were more prevalent in the young people who self-injured, especially among those who regularly experienced negativity and conflict in their family lives. The authors write: "These findings underscore the importance of considering both biological and environmental risk factors in understanding and treating self-injuring adolescents."[44]

Associated Psychiatric Disorders

Researchers now recognize a close association between self-injury disorder and mental illnesses such as borderline-personality disorder (BPD). The National Institute of Mental Health states that there is a high rate of self-injury among people with BPD. "A person with BPD may experience intense bouts of anger, depression, and anxiety that may last only hours, or at most a day. These may be associated with episodes of impulsive aggression, self-injury, and drug or alcohol abuse."[45] The American Self-Help Information Clearinghouse emphasizes, however, that not everyone with BPD resorts to self-injurious behavior. Although many mental health professionals automatically diagnose those who self-injure with BPD, all people who deliberately injure themselves do not suffer from the disorder.

Severe depression has also been linked with self-injury disorder. Although everyone feels sad or blue at times, and may even describe the feeling as "being depressed," that is not the same as clinical depression, which is a serious illness. Depression is caused by an alteration in brain chemistry that may be triggered by physical factors such as hormonal changes or disease or by psychological factors such as trauma or stress. People who suffer from severe depression live with a near-constant state of hopelessness and despair. A January 2009 article on the mental health Web site HealthyPlace explains:

> " Several studies have shown that people with self-injury disorder have an imbalance of serotonin, a chemical in the brain that serves as a regulator of emotions, appetite, and sleep. "

> For many victims of depression, these mental and physical feelings seem to follow them night and day, appear to have no end, and are not alleviated by happy events or good news. Some people are so disabled by feelings of despair that they cannot even build up the energy to call a doctor. If someone else calls for them, they may refuse to go because they are so hopeless that they think there's no point to it.[46]

People who suffer from depression may self-injure as a way to distract themselves from unbearable pain as well as to fight the urge to end their lives by committing suicide.

Another psychiatric illness that is common among those who self-injure is obsessive-compulsive disorder (OCD), which is an anxiety disorder. People with OCD are troubled by persistent and upsetting thoughts, or obsessions. In an effort to control the anxiety that these thoughts produce, they engage in ritualistic behaviors, or compulsions. Although not everyone with OCD engages in self-injury, some who have OCD may view self-injury as one of the rituals that they absolutely *must* perform.

> Another psychiatric illness that is common among those who self-injure is obsessive-compulsive disorder (OCD), which is an anxiety disorder.

For instance, one of Michael Hollander's OCD patients obsessively picked at the skin on her arms and legs. When the spots were healing, she picked off the scabs. She told Hollander that once she started picking at herself, she had no control over what she did and was unable to stop, and this scared her. He writes: "Frequently what drives the child's ritualistic behavior is some frightening idea that is accompanied by a powerful sense of dread. For example, she may feel that if she doesn't engage in the behavior, something awful will happen to a loved one."[47]

No Simple Answers

When people deliberately injure themselves, there are often multiple factors involved. Many have endured abuse or neglect as children or experienced some other type of traumatic event during childhood. If self-injury or other destructive behavior runs in someone's family, biology could play a role in whether he or she self-injures. Psychiatric illnesses such as depression, borderline personality disorder, and obsessive-compulsive disorder have also been linked to self-injury. These are all widely believed to be contributors to the development of self-injury disorder—but the exact cause? That remains a mystery.

Primary Source Quotes*

Why Do People Intentionally Injure Themselves?

66 Sometimes I feel dead. . . . When I cut, I know I'm real. I can see proof that I am still here. I can touch my blood, feel it pulsate out of me, and know that Vanessa, who-ever that is, is still here. 99

—Vanessa Vega, *Comes the Darkness, Comes the Light: A Memoir of Cutting, Healing, and Hope.* New York: AMACOM, 2007.

Vega is a high school English teacher and motivational speaker who has struggled with self-injury disorder for many years.

66 People who self-injure are no more psychotic than people who drown their sorrows in a bottle of liquor. 99

—Saskya Caicedo and Janis Whitlock, *Top 15 Misconceptions of Self-Injury*, 2008. www.crpsib.com.

Caicedo and Whitlock are with the Cornell University Research Program on Self-Injurious Behavior in Adolescents and Young Adults.

* Editor's Note: While the definition of a primary source can be narrowly or broadly defined, for the purposes of Compact Research, a primary source consists of: 1) results of original research presented by an organization or researcher; 2) eyewitness accounts of events, personal experience, or work experience; 3) first-person editorials offering pundits' opinions; 4) government officials presenting political plans and/or policies; 5) representatives of organizations presenting testimony or policy.

Primary Source Quotes

66 There are different theories as to why people self-mutilate. One is that because victims of childhood sexual abuse were forbidden to reveal the truth about their abuse, they use self-mutilation or self-cutting to express the horror of their abuse to the world. 99

—HealthyPlace, "Why People Self-Injure," September 22, 2009. www.healthyplace.com.

HealthyPlace is a Web site that specializes in mental health issues.

66 Like someone who's drowning, people who can't modulate their emotions flail about and reach for something to save them. Their self-harming behavior is the only life preserver they can find. 99

—Michael Hollander, *Helping Teens Who Cut*. New York: Guilford, 2008.

Hollander is a psychologist and an expert in the treatment of self-injury disorder.

66 The exact cause for self-injury is not completely established, although most researchers relate it to psychological issues. 99

—Goce Aleksovski, "Self Injury Answer A7063," Treating Self Injury, eHealth Forum, August 16, 2009. http://ehealthforum.com.

Aleksovski is a physician who specializes in family medicine and psychotherapy.

66 It starts as someone's solution to an emotional problem, but the solution can become more problematic than the original problem. The solution can take on a life of its own, and become like a runaway train. 99

—Sharon Farber, interviewed by David Roberts, "Getting Help for Self-Harm," HealthyPlace, April 11, 2007. www.healthyplace.com.

Farber is a therapist who specializes in self-injury disorder and is the author of *When the Body Is the Target: Self-Harm, Pain and Traumatic Attachments*.

“Using cutting to make yourself feel better is like using a one inch bandage on a wound that needs 100 stitches; the bandage is not enough.”

—Scott Wardell, “Cutting: Self-Injury Facts & Statistics,” ScottCounseling, February 6, 2009. www.scottcounseling.com.

Wardell is a therapist in Minneapolis, Minnesota.

“It has been reported that many people who self-injure have a history of sexual or physical abuse, but that is not always the case. Some may come from broken homes, alcoholic homes, have emotionally absent parents, etc. There are many factors that could cause someone to self-injure as a way to cope.”

—Colleen Thompson, “Self-Injury,” Mirror-Mirror, August 28, 2009. www.mirror-mirror.org.

Thompson is the editor of Mirror-Mirror, a Web site for people with eating disorders.

“Just as it’s suspected that the way the brain uses serotonin may play a role in depression, so scientists think that problems in the serotonin system may predispose some people to self-injury by making them tend to be more aggressive and impulsive than most people.”

—Deb Martinson, “Self-Injury: Fact Sheet (Beyond the Myths),” eNotAlone, 2009. www.enotalone.com.

Martinson is with the American Self-Harm Information Clearinghouse and the coauthor of *Secret Shame: Self-Injury Information and Support*.

“Self-injury also may be a reflection of a person’s self-hatred. Some self-injurers are punishing themselves for having strong feelings that they were usually not allowed to express as children. They also may be punishing themselves for somehow being bad and undeserving.”

—WebMD, “Mental Health and Self-Injury,” March 9, 2009. www.webmd.com.

WebMD provides health information, tools for managing health, and support to those who seek advice about health-related topics.

Facts and Illustrations

Why Do People Intentionally Injure Themselves?

- A study published in April 2007 by researchers from Harvard University and Boston University School of Medicine showed that **emotional and sexual abuse** were strongly linked with self-injury disorder, but there was not a significant connection with physical abuse or emotional neglect.

- Of the 10 girls William Shiels treated for embedding sharp objects into their skin, **40 percent** reported that they had been victims of sexual abuse.

- A study published in 2009 by researchers from the United Kingdom showed that **physical abuse,** rather than other kinds of childhood maltreatment, was significantly related to self-injury.

- According to a November 2008 article in the journal *Psychiatry*, up to **35 percent** of adult women diagnosed with anorexia, bulimia, and other eating disorders self-injure.

- An article that appeared in the July/August 2009 issue of *Comprehensive Psychiatry* reported that girls who had high levels of **nicotine dependence** were five times as likely as those who did not smoke to engage in self-injury.

- A study published in February 2008 showed that autistic children were **762 percent** more likely to be treated for self-inflicted injuries compared with children who did not have autism.

Self-Injury Risk Factors

Although an exact cause for self-injury disorder is unknown, those who specialize in treating patients who self-harm say that a number of contributors have been identified. This table shows some of the most common risk factors.

Biological Risk Factors	Environmental Risk Factors
Age (self-injury usually begins during adolescence when emotions are most volatile)	Emotional abuse and/or neglect
Mental health issues such as borderline personality disorder, obsessive-compulsive disorder, depression, post-traumatic stress disorder	Physical and/or sexual abuse
Genetic predisposition to high emotional/cognitive reactions	Hostile family environment: expression of feelings strongly discouraged and/or punished
Family history of suicide, self-injury, and/or other destructive behavior	Social isolation and living alone, unstable living conditions such as employment, divorce, death of a loved one

Sources: Matthew E. Nock, "Why Do People Hurt Themselves?" Harvard University, *Current Directions in Psychological Science*, 2009. www.wjh.harvard.edu; Mayo Clinic, "Self-Injury/Cutting," August 2, 2008. ww.mayoclinic.com.

- According to the Mayo Clinic, evidence suggests that self-injury is more common in people who have a family history of **suicide, self-injury, or self-destructive acts.**

- Research has shown a connection between self-injurious behavior and an imbalance in **serotonin,** a brain chemical that helps to regulate emotions and mood.

- Among those at highest risk for self-injuring are people who suffer from **mental illnesses** such as borderline personality disorder, obsessive-compulsive order, or severe depression.

The Role of Childhood Abuse

Not everyone who self-injures was abused as a child, and not all those who were abused resort to self-injury as a coping mechanism. But abuse has been shown to be a factor with many people who intentionally harm themselves. This graph shows how self-injurers attending college responded to a survey when asked about their childhood history.

Self-injurers who reported being physically, sexually, and/or emotionally abused as children

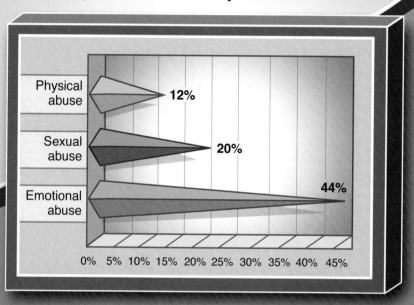

Source: Janis Whitlock, John Eckenrode, and Daniel Silverman, "Self-Injurious Behavior in a College Population," *Pediatrics*, June 2006. http://pediatrics.aappublications.org.

- Some researchers believe that people who self-injure may do so because of a desire to release **endorphins**, the body's natural opiate-like painkiller.

- Mental health professionals say that many who self-injure have been raised in an environment where **expressing private thoughts** and feelings is trivialized or harshly punished.

Self-Injury as an Addiction

One theory about the cause of self-injury disorder is that the first incident may be accidental and unplanned, but over time more acts of self-injury follow until the behavior becomes addictive. Although some psychotherapists do not believe that people can become addicted to injuring themselves, many who engage in self-harm disagree. This illustration shows the progressive process of self-injury under the addiction theory.

The progressive process of self-injury

The first incident of self-injury is accidental and/or impulsive

- The person experiences strong feelings such as anger, fear, or anxiety.
- The feelings continue to build until they are overwhelming; the person does not know how to express them.

Self-injury provides an immediate sense of relief

- The person experiences a reprieve from emotional pain, tension, and stress.
- Feelings of guilt and shame usually follow.
- In spite of the shame, the person has been "conditioned" to seek relief by self-injuring.

Strong feelings arise again, and the person feels emotionally overwhelmed

- In an effort to get rid of pain, the person again turns to self-injury, which is likely to increase in frequency and degree.
- The person becomes secretive about self-injurious acts, often hiding sharp objects or other tools, and concealing scars by wearing long sleeves and long pants.

After the self-injury, endorphins are released in the bloodstream

- Endorphins are the body's natural opiate-like painkillers, and the person may feel a sense of being high.
- Self-injury may become addictive because the person learns to associate it with the positive feelings caused by endorphins.

Source: Deborah Cutter, Jaelline Jaffe, and Jeanne Segal, "Cutting and Self-Injury," HelpGuide, February 2008. http://helpguide.org.

What Are the Prevention and Treatment Options for Self-Injurers?

"Of all disturbing patient behaviors, self-mutilation is often described as the most difficult for clinicians to understand and treat. Typically, these therapists and mental health practitioners are left feeling a combination of helplessness, horror, guilt, fury and sadness."

—Harry Croft, a psychiatrist and the medical director of HealthyPlace.

"There's no one best way to treat self-injury. . . . Treating self-injury can take time, hard work and your own desire to recover."

—The Mayo Clinic, a world-renowned medical facility headquartered in Rochester, Minnesota.

Because suicide is the third leading cause of death for 15- to 24-year-olds in the United States, suicide-prevention programs have been implemented in communities and schools throughout the country. But the same is not true of self-injury prevention. Despite the fact that self-injurers have a markedly high suicide risk and the number of young people who self-injure appears to be on the rise, programs that focus exclusively on prevention are rare to nonexistent. But as awareness of the prevalence—and the risks—of self-injury have increased, many health-care professionals are advocating for prevention programs. In a 2008 article in the *Journal of School Nursing*, registered nurse Sandra

Shapiro strongly urges school nurses to become better informed about self-injury and its associated risks and take measures to help prevent it. She writes: "Prevention strategies for all adolescents can be developed as well as strategies targeted at groups of at-risk adolescents. Because mental health care is critical for the treatment of self-injury, referral and early access to counseling is an important role for school nurses."[48]

Stopping Self-Injury Before It Happens

To address the need for preventive measures, a Wellesley Hills, Massachusetts–based group called Screening for Mental Health has created a program known as Signs of Self-Injury. It is the first program specifically designed for adolescents that attempts to increase knowledge, improve help-seeking attitudes and behaviors, and decrease incidents of self-injurious behavior. The focus is to teach high school students how to recognize the warning signs of depression or self-injury, either in themselves or in friends, and to respond effectively by seeking help from a trusted adult. They are taught to use an action-oriented approach known as Acknowledge, Care, and Tell, or ACT.

Psychologist Barent Walsh, who specializes in self-injury, was heavily involved in developing Signs of Self-Injury's content. According to Walsh, teaching young people healthy methods of handling emotions can play an important role in helping to prevent self-injury. He explains: "From a public health perspective, anything that enhances emotion regulation skills, coping skills, self-soothing skills would be something that would help prevent the onset of self-injury as a desperate attempt to manage emotional distress. . . . I think it has the potential to prevent some of this distress and bodily harm if people can learn these skills proactively."[49]

> " Despite the fact that self-injurers have a markedly high suicide risk and the number of young people who self-injure appears to be on the rise, programs that focus exclusively on prevention are rare to nonexistent. "

An article in the 2009 issue of *Journal of Youth and Adolescence* evaluated the Signs of Self-Injury program. It was implemented at five schools in Massachusetts and involved 274 high school students. After completion, the researchers examined pre- and post-evaluation surveys from the participants and interviewed guidance personnel who ran the program. Feedback from the students and educators showed that knowledge about self-injury had increased, as had attitudes toward seeking help. Overall, the effort was well-received by all those who participated, and it could prove to be an effective prevention strategy for many other schools.

The S.A.F.E. Alternatives Approach

Treatment programs that have been effective for many who self-injure revolve around intensive psychotherapy, which is intended to unlock the traumatic feelings that the person has kept buried inside. As Michelle Seliner explains: "It is our belief that once a client resolves underlying issues and learns to tolerate uncomfortable feelings rather than attempting to 'stuff' them, self-injury becomes unnecessary. It is also our experience that when a client gets healthier, self-injury becomes painful rather than helpful."[50] The primary focus of S.A.F.E. Alternatives is teaching patients skills that will help them control their emotions.

During counseling sessions patients learn to recognize irrational thoughts that could fuel anxiety and evoke intense feelings and reactions. They are reminded that the impulse to self-injure is a personal choice, rather than an addiction that cannot be controlled. Therapists help them create lists of alternatives to harming themselves, such as lighting candles, reading poetry, taking walks, or writing in a journal. The goal of engaging in these activities is to delay self-injury until the impulse to do so has been dulled.

Learning How to Cope

One type of outpatient treatment that has proved to be successful for many self-injurers is known as dialectical behavior therapy, or DBT. Developed by psychologist Marsha Linehan, DBT is one of the few treatments with clearly defined therapy techniques that are consistent from one mental health organization to another. Randi Kreger, who is the coauthor of *The Essential Family Guide to Borderline Personality Disorder*, says that DBT focuses on helping patients modify their ways of thinking and behaving. She explains: "The word 'dialectical' simply means that two opposite things can be true at the same time—in this case, that patients need to accept themselves, warts and all, yet recognize that by changing their destructive coping methods and learning other skills, they could have a better life."[51] Kreger adds that DBT has been shown to reduce the rate of self-injury, as well as suicide attempts, by as much as 50 percent compared with other types of therapy.

Patients who undergo DBT attend counseling sessions twice a week, once in a group and once in an individual session with a therapist. One focus is on distress tolerance, whereby patients learn how to cope with feelings of extreme anxiety in an appropriate manner. Therapist Michael Baugh explains: "I tell clients that Distress Tolerance is about getting through a crappy moment without doing something to make it worse."[52] An example of this is called "opposite action," which could involve doing something nice for someone who has made them angry rather than lashing out at the person. Another focus is on learning to control emotions in order to decrease the intensity of anger, fear, shame, and sadness. The third focus is known as interpersonal effectiveness, in which patients are taught ways of having a more positive outlook about themselves and their relationships with others.

> "Treatment programs that have been effective for many who self-injure revolve around intensive psychotherapy, which is intended to unlock the traumatic feelings that the person has kept buried inside."

Michael Hollander considers DBT to be the most effective type of therapy to help teenagers find ways other than self-injury to deal with their emotional vulnerabilities. He explains: "DBT directly targets the specific emotional and behavioral problems that plague the adolescent who deliberately self-injures. One of the key components of DBT is to teach these adolescents the relevant skills to handle their powerful emotional system. DBT is not a miracle treatment. It doesn't help everyone, but to date it's the best and fastest treatment there is."[53] Hollander adds that one of the main purposes of DBT is to help patients find other ways to calm and sooth themselves, rather than resorting to self-injury.

Altering a Way of Life

Because parents are typically frightened, and even angered, by a child's self-injurious behavior, their natural response is often to remove all sharp objects from a home. Many therapists have also told patients that they must turn over their razor blades before starting treatment. This is often counterproductive, however, because it can intensify the person's feelings of helplessness and lack of control. Sharon Farber shares her thoughts: "I think if the person gives up the cutting before they are ready to do it, psychologically, they will find some other ways to hurt themselves or find other people to do it. So before someone gives up their cutting implements they need to think about whether they are ready to do this or not."[54]

Farber adds that making the decision to give up a coping mechanism that has helped someone deal with extreme pain can make the person feel desperate: "Forbidden fruit always tastes sweeter. When you give something up, it makes you yearn for it more." She says that getting beyond self-injury is more than giving up a certain behavior. It is about giving up a way of life that has been attached to emotional pain and suffering, "and when this happens, the self-injury falls by the wayside because it is not needed."[55]

> One type of outpatient treatment that has proved to be successful for many self-injurers is known as dialectical behavior therapy, or DBT.

Like Farber, Meryl Quinn says that attempts to stop people from self-injuring, such as hiding sharp objects, will inevitably fail. Quinn has been cutting herself since she was about 12 years old. Today her self-injury episodes are sporadic; she may go for long periods of time without cutting, and then cut herself on a daily basis if she is suffering from emotional distress. She writes:

> You may . . . have the feeling that you should take away
> all the knives and blades so they are not accessible. This

won't stop a cutter who is intent on cutting. We are resourceful, if nothing else. We will use paper clips that have been straightened out, staples, nail clippers, nail files, our fingernails, whatever we have to. It would be impossible in other words to remove everything a cutter could use to hurt themselves.[56]

Quinn adds that if those who want to self-injure are deprived of ways of doing so, it only makes matters worse. "We tend to carry a sharp object with us, but can improvise when we have to. Taking away our pocket knife or nail clippers will probably just cause panic and create a situation where we feel out of control. That is when we grab whatever is handy and wing it."[57]

Ruta Mazelis agrees that trying to force someone to stop engaging in self-injurious behavior is futile. Referring to it as self-inflicted violence (SIV), she says this is true not only of removing sharp objects, but also hospitalizing the person without his or her consent. She writes:

> Currently professional emphasis remains on efforts to stop self-injuring behavior at all cost. . . . Most people are angered, frightened, or disgusted by our behavior, including many in the mental health community. Interventions such as forced hospitalization, restraint and seclusion (being tied down or locked in isolation rooms), mandated medications . . . are coercive and retraumatizing. While they might make us stop SIV in the moment, they reenact our original loss of power and control and ultimately do more harm than good.[58]

Mazelis, like numerous others who specialize in self-injury, emphasizes the importance of self-injurers working through the trauma that is at the core of their problems. Only by doing that can healing occur.

The Myth of Attention Seeking

Crucial components in whether people can overcome self-injury are compassion and understanding—which self-injurers unfortunately do not encounter very often. As erroneous as it may be, the prevailing belief about those who deliberately harm themselves is that they are manipulative people who self-injure in order to bring attention to themselves. Quinn shares her thoughts about how wrong this perception is:

> Cutting is *not* about getting attention. Most cutters are very secretive about their activities. This is understandable as few people can be understanding about it and some will react in ways that make the cutter feel even worse. I remember when I first "came out" about my cutting. My aunt thought it would be a good idea to try to have a loud conversation about it at a family gathering. Shame is the last thing a cutter needs. In fact, you can trigger an episode if you create a difficult enough situation for the cutter to handle emotionally.[59]

According to Hollander, studies have suggested that less than 4 percent of adolescents deliberately hurt themselves to get attention, but it is still "the most common reason that parents and some therapists give to account for the behavior—despite the fact that often an adolescent is self-injuring for months before an adult even notices."[60] One of Hollander's patients was a 13-year-old girl named Erin, who had been hospitalized a number of times for self-injury and suicidal thoughts. Her psychiatrist said that she had been cutting herself for the past 2 years, but that her parents had only found out about it 8 months before. Hollander asked the psychiatrist his opinion about why Erin injured herself, and the man confidently expressed that she was doing it to get attention. Hollander was perplexed by this, as he explains: "How could a young girl be seeking attention through a behavior that she kept secret for well over a year? When I posed this question to the psychiatrist, he realized immediately that he may have leapt too quickly to his conclusion."[61]

> Crucial components in whether people can overcome self-injury are compassion and understanding—which self-injurers unfortunately do not encounter very often.

Hope for the Future

Although a number of treatment methods have proved to be effective at helping self-injurers stop deliberately harming themselves, preventive measures are still in their infancy. As awareness of self-injury increases, the myths surrounding it may eventually be dispelled, and people will develop a better understanding of the emotional turmoil that leads to it. If that happens, there may be greater focus on preventing self-injury before it starts.

What Are the Prevention and Treatment Options for Self-Injurers?

"One danger connected with self-injury is that it tends to become an addictive behavior, a habit that is difficult to break even when the individual wants to stop."

—Deborah Cutter, Jaelline Jaffe, and Jeanne Segal, "Cutting and Self-Injury," HelpGuide, February 2008. http://helpguide.org.

Cutter, Jaffe, and Segal are all psychologists in California.

"While some of our clients have been diagnosed with psychiatric disorders which may need to be managed over their lifetime, we do not view the behavior of self-injury as an addiction."

—Michelle Seliner, interviewed by Natalie, "Treating Self-Injury," HealthyPlace, April 11, 2007. www.healthyplace.com.

Seliner is a therapist and the chief operating officer for the S.A.F.E. Alternatives treatment program.

Bracketed quotes indicate conflicting positions.

* Editor's Note: While the definition of a primary source can be narrowly or broadly defined, for the purposes of Compact Research, a primary source consists of: 1) results of original research presented by an organization or researcher; 2) eyewitness accounts of events, personal experience, or work experience; 3) first-person editorials offering pundits' opinions; 4) government officials presenting political plans and/or policies; 5) representatives of organizations presenting testimony or policy.

❝The reality is that I have gone from cutting four or more times a day to only once or twice a year. It is my hope that as I continue to work to better understand myself, there will come a day when I don't cut at all.❞

—Vanessa Vega, *Comes the Darkness, Comes the Light: A Memoir of Cutting, Healing, and Hope*. New York: AMACOM, 2007.

Vega is a high school English teacher and motivational speaker who has struggled with self-injury disorder for many years.

❝The good news with self-injury coming out of the closet is that researchers began to study the problem in an attempt both to understand it and to develop more effective treatments.❞

—Michael Hollander, *Helping Teens Who Cut*. New York: Guilford, 2008.

Hollander is a psychologist and an expert in the treatment of self-injury disorder.

❝Self injury is not treated as a separate syndrome, and so there are few specific ways of reducing self injury. Treatments tend to focus on the whole person, and on the underlying causes of stress and anxiety.❞

—LifeSIGNS (Self Injury Guidance & Network Support), "Self Injury Awareness Booklet," eNotAlone, 2009. www.enotalone.com.

LifeSIGNS is a voluntary organization based in the United Kingdom that aims to support all people who are affected in any way by self-injury.

❝Refusing to give anesthesia for stitches, making disparaging remarks, and treating the patient as an inconvenient nuisance simply further the feelings of invalidation and unworthiness the self-injurer already feels.❞

—Deb Martinson, "Self-Injury: Fact Sheet (Beyond the Myths)," eNotAlone, 2009. www.enotalone.com.

Martinson is with the American Self-Harm Information Clearinghouse and the coauthor of *Secret Shame: Self-Injury Information and Support*.

66 Most people, even some who live with SIV [self-inflicted violence], focus almost completely on making SIV go away, as if it were an evil to be eradicated, after which there would be peace for all. This attitude is understandable, yet it has caused incomprehensible suffering for many who have lived with SIV. 99

—Ruta Mazelis, "You'll Stop When It's Time," Healing Self-Injury, December 8, 2008. http://healingselfinjury.org.

Mazelis is a content specialist for Sidran Traumatic Stress Institute on self-harming behaviors and related issues and is the creator of the Healing Self-Injury blog and the *Cutting Edge* newsletter.

66 The standard treatment for self-injury involves focusing on emotional regulation through skills training. Clients are taught to pay attention to the irrational thoughts that might serve to fuel intensive feeling states. They are also taught to focus on the present rather than the past. 99

—S.A.F.E. Alternatives, "Who We Are: FAQ," 2007. www.selfinjury.com.

Self Abuse Finally Ends (S.A.F.E.) Alternatives is a nationally recognized treatment program designed for people who self-injure.

Facts and Illustrations

What Are the Prevention and Treatment Options for Self-Injurers?

- A 2009 study published in the *Journal of Youth and Adolescence* reported that a **prevention program** involving 274 adolescents at five schools resulted in increased knowledge about self-injury and improved help-seeking attitudes and intentions among students.

- According to a 2007 report by psychologists from Cornell University, a study about Internet discussion groups showed that **37 percent** of respondents believed such forums had helped with their efforts to stop self-injuring.

- A November 2008 article in the journal *Psychiatry* cited a study that found **70 percent** of teenagers who engage in self-injury had made at least one suicide attempt, and **55 percent** had made multiple attempts.

- It is well known that many who self-injure do not seek treatment, because many keep their behavior a secret. This was confirmed in a 2008 survey of nearly 1,000 people from the United Kingdom, in which **84 percent** said they hid their self-injury from their families and 66 percent said they tried to hide it from friends.

- A 2008 study of nearly 3,000 college students revealed that **7 percent** had engaged in self-injury within the past 4 weeks, but only **26 percent** of those had sought therapy or medication.

A Successful Prevention Strategy

Although there is no guaranteed way to prevent people from developing self-injury disorder, steps can be taken to reduce the risk. The Mayo Clinic states that prevention strategies may need to involve individuals as well as communities and include parents, schools, health-care professionals, and coaches, among others. This table shows some techniques that may help prevent young people from heading down the path of self-injurious behavior.

Methods of potentially preventing self-injury

Raising awareness

- Adults, especially those who work with young people, need to be educated about the warning signs of self-injury, such as someone wearing long-sleeve shirts and/or jackets during hot weather.
- Adults also should know what to do if they suspect that someone self-injures.

Identifying those who are most at risk and offering help

- Recognize high-risk individuals and help them learn healthy coping skills.
- During periods of distress or emotional pain, they may draw on the skills rather than turning to self-injury in order to cope.

Expanding social networks

- Many who self-injure feel lonely and disconnected from family and peers.
- Helping them to form connections with others can improve their relationship and communication skills.

Promoting programs that encourage peers to seek help

- Peers are often loyal to friends, even if they know someone is self-injuring.
- Programs that encourage young people to reach out to trusted adults may teach them that keeping self-injurious behavior a secret may hurt their friends rather than help them.

Offering education about the influence of the media

- News media, music, television programs, Web sites, and other highly visible outlets that feature self-injury may encourage vulnerable young people to experiment with it themselves.
- If children are taught critical thinking skills about the potential influence of the media, this may discourage them from becoming involved with self-injury.

Source: Mayo Clinic, "Self-Injury/Cutting," August 2, 2008. www.mayoclinic.com.

A Successful Treatment Strategy

A number of psychotherapists treat self-injurers with a method known as dialectical behavior therapy, or DBT, with which many patients have made excellent progress. One example is the Adolescent Dialectical Behavior program at the Two Brattle Center facility in Cambridge, Massachusetts. This graph shows participants' responses to questions in the two weeks before DBT treatment, compared with the last two weeks of treatment.

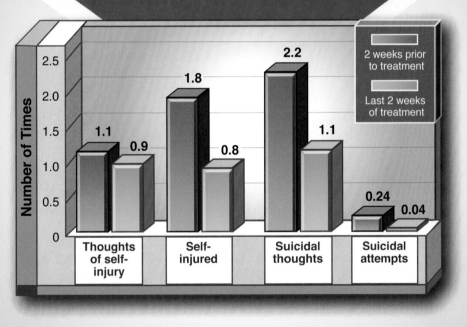

Average number of times reported of each behavior, two weeks before dialectical behavior therapy versus last two weeks of treatment

Number of Times

	2 weeks prior to treatment	Last 2 weeks of treatment
Thoughts of self-injury	1.1	0.9
Self-injured	1.8	0.8
Suicidal thoughts	2.2	1.1
Suicidal attempts	0.24	0.04

Source: Michael Hollander, *Helping Teens Who Cut.* New York: Guilford Press, 2008, p. 195.

- An August 2008 report by the Centers for Disease Control and Prevention showed that intentional injuries accounted for about **2.5 million** visits to hospital emergency rooms during 2006.

A Residential Program Shows Results

A residential treatment facility in Westborough, Massachusetts, has a goal of completely eliminating self-injurious behavior through intensive dialectical behavior therapy, or DBT. A study published in 2008 compared two groups of patients: those who had participated in two or more rounds of DBT, and those who received one round or less. Although both groups made progress, the patients who received two or more rounds of DBT reported a more significant reduction in self-injury.

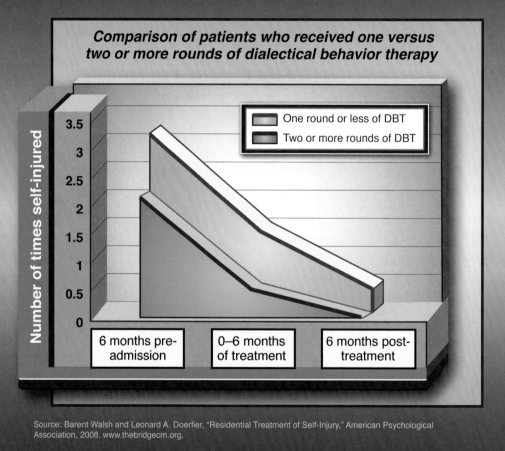

Comparison of patients who received one versus two or more rounds of dialectical behavior therapy

One round or less of DBT
Two or more rounds of DBT

Number of times self-injured

6 months pre-admission
0–6 months of treatment
6 months post-treatment

Source: Barent Walsh and Leonard A. Doerfler, "Residential Treatment of Self-Injury," American Psychological Association, 2008. www.thebridgecm.org.

- The National Institute of Mental Health states that, compared with other kinds of therapy, a treatment called **dialectical behavior therapy** reduced suicide attempts by half in people with borderline personality disorder, which is closely associated with self-injurious behavior.

Can People Overcome Self-Injury Disorder?

> 66 The good news is that people can and do get better all the time and go on to live healthy, productive lives. 99

—Michelle Seliner, a therapist and chief operating officer for the S.A.F.E. Alternatives treatment program.

> 66 I basically think that cutters are never 'cured.' We are like alcoholics, who drink to cope; the urge is usually there under the surface waiting for something to happen. 99

—Meryl Quinn, a business development director for a health and wellness company, who has self-injured since she was 12 years old.

Connie Hanagan is a survivor—although she went through many years of excruciating pain before she reached this point. Hanagan's self-injury began when she was in the fourth grade and life presented her with problems that, at her young age, seemed insurmountable. Love and affection were rarely shown in her strict family, and she never told anyone that she had been sexually molested when she was seven years old. In addition, school was difficult for her because she had a hearing deficiency as well as dyslexia, a learning disability. In an effort to deal with what she perceived as unbearable emotional trauma, she started cutting herself with razor blades and shards of glass. "I needed a release," she says. "I hated myself."[62]

> Because self-injurious behavior is so often the result of deep, internalized pain, many people who suffer from it cannot recover without professional guidance.

After eight or nine years of self-injury, Hanagan was diagnosed with schizophrenia, a psychotic disorder, and was labeled a troublemaker. She spent time in hospitals, but nothing seemed to help her because no one understood what she was going through. To make things worse, hospital staff seemed to have no idea how to deal with people who deliberately injured themselves. She explains: "Nobody knows why anyone does this. I was hurting inside. Cutting was a release; a way of letting the pain out."[63] Hanagan says that what would have helped her back then was someone who showed understanding, concern, and love, but this was not her experience. Instead, she felt as though she had no one to turn to for support.

When she was in her twenties, Hanagan was finally able to stop cutting. She says that in large part, this was simply due to growing up and becoming mature. She explains: "I began to find my voice, and to confide in some people about myself."[64] Many years have passed since she deliberately harmed herself. And although her physical scars remain, she believes she is free from the underlying trauma that once caused her such emotional anguish.

Stories of Recovery

Because self-injurious behavior is so often the result of deep, internalized pain, many people who suffer from it cannot recover without professional guidance. Only through intensive therapy do they develop the courage to face the emotional demons that have long plagued them. This was the case with Brittany Burden, who found herself on a downward spiral after cutting herself for seven years. She spent four days in the hospital and left believing that she was cured—then soon realized how wrong she was, as she writes: "I walked out of the hospital a healthier, happier woman. But this wasn't the end of my story; you can't be cured in four days."[65]

Almost immediately after her release, Burden went right back to cutting herself. She began making even deeper wounds than she had before, using any sharp object she could get her hands on. She also found herself wondering when the day would finally come that she would try to take her own life. Realizing that she desperately needed help, Burden began doing research on available treatments for self-injury, and in the process she learned about the S.A.F.E. Alternatives program. She found a treatment center located in Denton, Texas, and in spite of the short notice, she was immediately accepted as a patient.

At first Burden was so terrified that she cried herself to sleep at night. But it was not long before she began to feel more comfortable at the facility, and she made friends with other patients whom she refers to as her "new family." She writes: "We all came together in those 30 days, laughing, learning and sharing our injuries and experiences." Throughout her month of inpatient and outpatient therapy, Burden made remarkable progress: "My days in S.A.F.E. were something like the very best of my life. They were the beginning of the end of a seven-year battle with self-injury. . . . I learned to set boundaries with friends and family, to stand up for myself, to be open about my emotions, to cry unabashedly, to make a new family where my other was shaken, and to be myself at all costs."[66]

Another success story is Donna Nagy, who had been cutting herself with razors, scissors, and pencils since she was 12 years old. She was diagnosed with depression, and at the beginning of her eighth-grade year, she tried to commit suicide by overdosing on antidepressants. After a short hospitalization Donna entered the S.A.F.E. Alternatives program and completed it in 30 days. She says she learned many things about herself that she did not know before. Now, for the first time, Donna is confident that she no longer needs to self-injure, as she explains: "Now that I've gone through all the treatment, I've realized I'm better than this. . . . There's nothing in the world that's bad enough that would give you a reason to harm yourself—like a real reason."[67]

Determined to Self-Heal

Although many people who self-injure cannot stop doing it without professional help, some fight the battle on their own—and win. Hanagan is one example, and she largely attributes her recovery from self-injury to teaching herself healthier ways of coping with pain. She found that she no longer needed to cut herself in order to deal with overwhelming emotions. She explains: "When something bothers me, I don't hurt myself. I cry."[68]

Others have successfully healed themselves as well. A March 1, 2008, article in the *Charleston Gazette* focused on several students at West Virginia's South Charleston High School. Although the teenagers wished to remain anonymous, they were willing to talk freely about their self-injurious behavior. One boy said that he had started cutting himself as a form of self-punishment because he "felt worthless"[69] and was filled with self-blame. He also got involved with drugs such as cocaine, which only deepened his feelings of hopelessness and despair. But one day he suddenly realized that he had a serious problem, and rather than keeping it inside, he turned to a close friend for help. The friend was supportive, saying that he would do everything he could to help, and the boy knew that he could confide in his friend whenever he needed to—which helped him overcome the need to cut himself. He encourages others to seek out trusted friends who are willing to support them: "People need to learn that there are ways out of [cutting] and other ways to deal with problems."[70]

> **Although many people who self-injure cannot stop doing it without professional help, some fight the battle on their own—and win.**

Another teenager who was interviewed for the *Gazette* story says that she started self-injuring because she was depressed and generally unhappy with her life. She explains: "My dad was abusive, and I had really low self-worth. Everything was happening at once. My great grandma died, and my boyfriend broke up with me. I felt like cutting was the only way to get rid of the pain . . . but the pain, no matter what, was still there."[71] She says that what caused her to stop injuring herself was a radical change in attitude: "I finally quit because I realized it was pointless, and I wasn't getting anything out of it at all. Life is going to go on no matter what, and cutting isn't going to help it any."[72]

Like her male classmate, the girl also turned to close friends for help, and they "snapped me back into real life. They showed me that I don't really need to do that because it's not worth it. It all kind of happened pretty quickly." She never considered seeking professional help because she did not believe it would be beneficial. She explains: "You don't feel like you're going to get enough support from [psychotherapists] because they're like every other doctor—they're seeing several other people at the same time; they're just doing their job."[73] With her friends, however, she found the support that she so badly needed. They listened to her whenever she needed to talk. They helped her stay strong by encouraging her not to return to self-injury, which was a major factor in why she stopped cutting herself.

Getting the Word Out

Because of all the myths and misconceptions surrounding self-injury disorder, several organizations are making a concerted effort to educate the public. One is the American Self-Harm Information Clearinghouse (ASHIC), which was founded by Deb Martinson. Its goal is to dispel myths about self-injury, as well as to improve the treatment of those who self-harm by hospitals, physicians, psychotherapists, family, and friends. The group has developed fact sheets, brochures, and a "bill of rights" for those who self-harm, which is designed to enable health-care professionals to understand more clearly the emotions that underlie self-injury and to respond to self-injurious behavior in a way that is most beneficial to patients.

One of ASHIC's major projects is the creation of the National Self-Injury Awareness Day, which is a grassroots educational and awareness effort. Every year on March 1 people throughout the United States and several other countries distribute informational packets to a variety of locations. These include hospital emergency rooms and psychiatric wards, school guidance counseling offices, university counseling services, psychotherapists' offices, and crisis line operations, as well as anywhere else that could benefit from accurate information about self-injury. Mark Lepore, who is clinical coordinator for the counseling center at Clarion University in Pennsylvania, explains the importance of such efforts to increase knowledge about self-injury: "The first step toward coping with

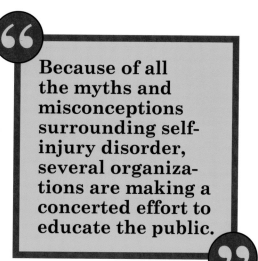

> **Because of all the myths and misconceptions surrounding self-injury disorder, several organizations are making a concerted effort to educate the public.**

self-injurious behavior is education: bringing reliable information about who self-injures, why they do it, and how they can learn to stop."[74]

Those Who Cannot Recover

Although many people feel as though they have overcome self-injury and have every intention of never harming themselves again, mental health professionals often find that their patients are unable to stop. According to Michelle Seliner, it is not at all unusual for these people to relapse. No matter how badly self-injurers may want to stop, they find it difficult—even terrifying—to give up the only coping mechanism that has ever worked for them. A young woman who posted on a self-injury forum in October 2009 spoke of her feelings of hopelessness, fear, and despair when she tried to stop cutting herself: "It's been a couple of months and I'm breaking down. I can't go on without leaving one more scar on my wrist. It's so hard to put up with the emotional abuse I go through. . . . For those of you who haven't cut, don't. The urges are bad and it'll kill you. I just want to hold a knife to my wrist until I bleed to death."[75]

> **She never considered seeking professional help because she did not believe it would be beneficial.**

Andrew Daniel Evans understands what this young woman is going through. Evans has been a self-injurer for four years. He has been through therapy and has been hospitalized three times because of self-injury relapses, and still he continues to cut himself. He explains how difficult quitting is for him or anyone else who tries: "Unlike 'habits,' self-mutilation is not so easily cured. It's an addiction and a disease as horrible as alcoholism and drug addiction."[76]

A Lifelong Struggle

Overcoming self-injurious behavior is often a difficult and frightening task for those who live with it every day. Some people have found the strength and courage to stop on their own, while others have felt that they were unable to do so without professional help. Many have believed that they have overcome the need to self-injure, only to return to doing it again. For them, self-injury might very well be a lifelong battle.

Burden considers herself one of the fortunate ones. Since her release from the S.A.F.E. Alternatives treatment program in 2008, she has not intentionally injured herself, and she is convinced that she has recovered. "Though it still feels overwhelming," she writes, "I carry on. Real life is a strange and unnerving journey through even more strange and unnerving events. But there's nothing to do but carry on. I cannot stop my life, and I no longer want to."[77]

Primary Source Quotes*

Can People Overcome Self-Injury Disorder?

66 With proper treatment, new ways of coping will be learned and slowly the cycle of hurting will end. 99

—Deborah Serani, "March 1st Is Self-Injury Awareness Day," Dr. Deb's blog, February 26, 2007. http://drdeborahserani.blogspot.com.

Serani is a psychologist who specializes in trauma and depression.

66 The prognosis for self-injury varies depending upon a person's emotional or psychological state. It is important to determine the factors that lead [to] an individual's self-injuring behaviors. It also is important to identify any pre-existing personality disorders that need to be treated. 99

—Amal Chakraburtty, "Mental Health and Self-Injury," WebMD, March 9, 2009. www.webmd.com.

Chakraburtty is a psychiatrist in Oklahoma.

* Editor's Note: While the definition of a primary source can be narrowly or broadly defined, for the purposes of Compact Research, a primary source consists of: 1) results of original research presented by an organization or researcher; 2) eyewitness accounts of events, personal experience, or work experience; 3) first-person editorials offering pundits' opinions; 4) government officials presenting political plans and/or policies; 5) representatives of organizations presenting testimony or policy.

❝I have made it a personal goal of mine that I will NEVER self injure again. I've gained so much in this year, and I've worked too hard to throw it all away.❞

—Emily J., "Recovering from Self-Injury," HealthyPlace, February 6, 2009. www.healthyplace.com.

Emily is a young woman who battled self-injury disorder for many years.

❝The scars were thick and purple, but over the years, they've turned thin and white. You can barely see them, except in the summer when I get tan, and then they rise to the surface, like lace on my skin.❞

—Robert Goolrick, *The End of the World as We Know It*. Chapel Hill, NC: Algonquin, 2007.

Goolrick stopped self-injuring after cutting himself for much of his life.

❝I have learned that the past has only as much power as I give it. It has shaped the person I *am*, but it does not have to dictate the person I will *be!*❞

—Vanessa Vega, *Comes the Darkness, Comes the Light: A Memoir of Cutting, Healing, and Hope*. New York: AMACOM, 2007.

Vega is a high school English teacher and motivational speaker who has struggled with self-injury disorder for many years.

❝People stop living with SIV [self-inflicted violence] when they no longer need it, when the reasons they turned to it in the first place are in the process of being healed, and when they expand their options for managing them.❞

—Ruta Mazelis, "Frequently Asked Questions," Healing Self-Injury blog, May 2008. http://healingselfinjury.org.

Mazelis is a content specialist for Sidran Traumatic Stress Institute on self-harming behaviors and related issues and is the creator of the Healing Self-Injury blog and the *Cutting Edge* newsletter.

---

66 I think getting beyond self-injury is more than giving up a certain behavior. It's about giving up a way of life that is attached to pain and suffering, emotional pain and emotional suffering, and when this happens, the self-injury falls by the wayside because it is not needed. 99

—Sharon Farber, interviewed by David Roberts, "Getting Help for Self-Harm," HealthyPlace, April 11, 2007. www.healthyplace.com.

Farber is a therapist who specializes in self-injury disorder and is the author of *When the Body Is the Target: Self-Harm, Pain and Traumatic Attachments*.

66 Unless there is significant neurological damage, we don't believe that people can't control or learn to stop self-injury. . . . They may still experience intense emotional states, but they can learn to respond in a healthier, more productive way. 99

—S.A.F.E. Alternatives, "Who We Are," 2007. www.selfinjury.com.

Self Abuse Finally Ends (S.A.F.E.) Alternatives is a nationally recognized treatment program designed for people who self-injure.

66 Until society dispels all the myths surrounding self-injury and . . . educate themselves on this subject, sufferers will continue to keep quiet and this form of abuse will continue to be a secret for a long time to come. 99

—Colleen Thompson, "Self-Injury," Mirror-Mirror, August 28, 2009. www.mirror-mirror.org.

Thompson is the editor of Mirror-Mirror, a Web site for people with eating disorders.

Facts and Illustrations

Can People Overcome Self-Injury Disorder?

- One study showed that **75 percent** of the patients who completed the S.A.F.E. Alternatives program remained injury free two years after their discharge.

- Some studies have reported that when self-injury is accompanied by depression, **antidepressant drugs** may help the person overcome the urge to self-injure.

- According to the group To Write Love on Her Arms, **two-thirds** of the people suffering from depression never seek treatment; if they self-injure, this could make it extremely difficult to overcome the behavior.

- Some people say one of the major reasons they are unable to stop self-injuring is because they feel **addicted to the practice,** much like those who are addicted to alcohol and drugs.

- The S.A.F.E. Alternatives treatment program strongly discourages the use of anti-anxiety medications because if patients are to overcome self-injury, they need to acknowledge that they have the **ability to tolerate** and work through the anxiety, rather than suppressing it with drugs.

Substitutes for Self-Injury

Some people who have overcome self-injury have found it helpful to use substitute methods of dealing with emotional pain, such as slashing a plastic soda bottle instead of cutting their skin, snapping their wrists with rubber bands, or drawing on their arms and legs with a red marker to simulate blood. But in a poll on the S.A.F.E. Alternatives Web site, most of the participants who had used alternative methods did not find them helpful in reducing self-injury, and nearly 50 percent said their desire to self-injure increased, as this chart shows.

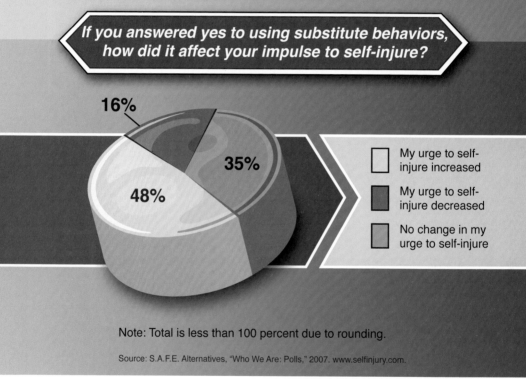

If you answered yes to using substitute behaviors, how did it affect your impulse to self-injure?

16%

35%

48%

☐ My urge to self-injure increased

☐ My urge to self-injure decreased

☐ No change in my urge to self-injure

Note: Total is less than 100 percent due to rounding.

Source: S.A.F.E. Alternatives, "Who We Are: Polls," 2007. www.selfinjury.com.

- A report published in the November 2007 issue of the *Journal of Clinical Psychology* states that most adolescent self-injurers who receive **help and support** do not become lifelong self-harmers.

- According to psychologist Michael Hollander, adolescents who participated in a Massachusetts **dialectical behavior therapy** program reported a significant decrease in thoughts of self-injury, self-injurious behavior, and suicidal thoughts.

Most Self-Injurers Do Not Seek Help

Various types of treatment programs have helped self-injurers overcome the desire to harm themselves. But many self-injurers never seek treatment. This became apparent during a survey of college students by psychologists from Cornell University. Nearly 500 of the 2,875 participants defined themselves as having practiced self-injury at some time in their lives, but most never sought professional help.

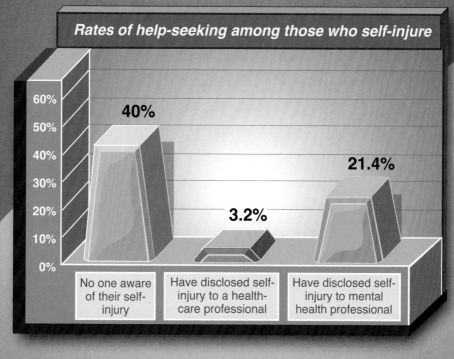

Rates of help-seeking among those who self-injure

40%	**3.2%**	**21.4%**
No one aware of their self-injury	Have disclosed self-injury to a health-care professional	Have disclosed self-injury to mental health professional

Source: Janice Whitlock, John Eckenrode, and Daniel Silverman, "Self-Injurious Behavior in a College Population," *Pediatrics*, June 2006. http://pediatrics.aappublications.org.

- S.A.F.E. Alternatives states that people who stop self-injuring on their own without therapy may be at risk for **switching to another way of coping,** such as drugs or alcohol.

Self-Harm and the Internet

Studies have shown that those who self-injure are increasingly turning to the Web to find support and understanding. Online discussion groups in particular have been singled out as extremely helpful. This chart shows how members on one Web-based support group responded to an online questionnaire about their involvement in the group.

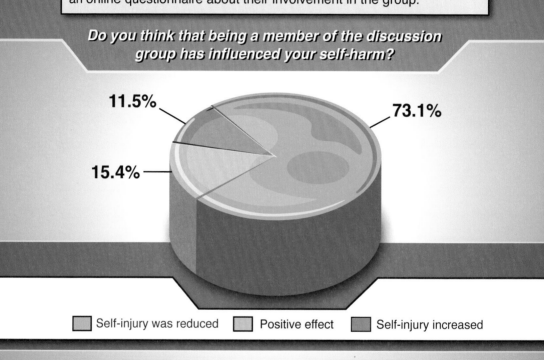

Do you think that being a member of the discussion group has influenced your self-harm?

11.5%

73.1%

15.4%

☐ Self-injury was reduced ☐ Positive effect ☐ Self-injury increased

Source: Craig D. Murray and Jezz Fox, "Do Internet Discussion Groups Alleviate or Exacerbate Self-Harming Behavior?" *Australian e-Journal for the Advancement of Mental Health*, December 2006. www.auseinet.com.

- Psychologists Janis Whitlock, Wendy Lader, and Karen Conterio state that **social networking sites** aid recovery by helping self-injurers feel less isolated and more connected with their peers.

- A survey of self-injurers published in the July 2008 issue of the *Journal of Mental Health Counseling* showed that **81 percent** said that it was helpful to know that someone was available to assist them if they needed it.

- A study published in the February 2007 issue of the *American Journal of Psychiatry* found that **physical exercise** significantly decreased the frequency of self-injury in one patient who had harmed herself for 13 years.

- According to the Summer 2009 issue of the *Child Health Literature Review* newsletter, studies have shown that **80 to 90 percent** of patients who undergo dialectical behavior therapy recover from self-injurious behavior.

Key People and Advocacy Groups

American Self-Harm Information Clearinghouse: An organization that strives to educate the general public as well as health-care professionals about self-injury.

Karen Conterio and Wendy Lader: The cofounders of the Self Abuse Finally Ends (S.A.F.E.) Alternatives treatment program and nationally recognized experts on self-injury.

Cornell Research Program on Self-Injurious Behavior: A program affiliated with Cornell University that conducts research on self-injurious behavior and furnishes its research findings to anyone who is affected by self-injury.

Sharon Farber: A psychologist who specializes in self-injury disorder and is the author of the book *When the Body Is the Target: Self-Harm, Pain and Traumatic Attachments.*

Armando Favazza: A psychiatrist and author of *Bodies Under Siege: Self-Mutilation in Culture and Psychiatry,* which was published in 1987 and was the first in-depth psychological book about self-harm.

Michael Hollander: A psychotherapist who specializes in self-injury and is the author of the book *Helping Teens Who Cut.*

Marsha Linehan: A psychologist who developed the dialectical behavior therapy, or DBT, approach to treating people with borderline personality and/or self-injury disorder.

Key People and Advocacy Groups

Deb Martinson: A former self-injurer who founded the American Self-Harm Information Clearinghouse.

Ruta Mazelis: A content specialist for Sidran Traumatic Stress Institute on self-harming behaviors and related issues.

S.A.F.E. Alternatives: The only inpatient treatment facility in the United States that is specifically devoted to helping people who self-injure.

Self Injury Foundation: A group that provides research funding, advocacy, support, and education for those who self-injure as well as their families and the health-care professionals who work with them.

Michelle Seliner: A psychotherapist and the chief operating officer for the S.A.F.E. Alternatives treatment program.

William Shiels: The chief of radiology at Nationwide Children's Hospital in Columbus, Ohio, who advocates the adoption of self-embedding disorder as an official psychiatric diagnosis.

Janis Whitlock: A psychologist and the director of Cornell University's Self-Injurious Behavior in Adolescents and Young Adults research program.

Chronology

Chronology

1952

The first edition of the *Diagnostic and Statistical Manual of Mental Disorders* is published by the American Psychiatric Association, ushering in the formal classification of modern mental illnesses.

1875

American psychiatrist Walter Channing treats a 30-year-old mental hospital patient and removes at least 150 objects from her body, including glass shards, splinters of wood, needles, pins, nails, and a piece of tin. Channing notes that the woman reportedly felt no pain as she injured herself.

1987

Psychiatrist Armando Favazza publishes *Bodies Under Siege: Self-Mutilation in Culture and Psychiatry*, which is the first in-depth psychological book about self-harm.

1938

Psychiatrist Karl Menninger publishes *Man Against Himself*, a book that describes self-injury as a way to soothe oneself and as an act of self-preservation, rather than an attempt to commit suicide.

1875   **1950**   **1990**

1913

Self-injury first appears in psychological literature with the publication of L.E. Emerson's "The Case of Miss A," which is the account of a young woman with a childhood history of sexual and physical abuse who repeatedly cut her legs and arms.

1965

In a study by researcher O. Ivar Lovaas and his colleagues, researchers find that they are able to control the frequency of self-injury by manipulating social consequences. They learn that positive reinforcement increases the frequency of self-injury, whereas ignoring the behavior decreases the frequency.

1986

The Program for the Treatment of Self Injury is cofounded by psychotherapists Karen Conterio and Wendy Lader. Its name is later changed to Self Abuse Finally Ends (S.A.F.E.) Alternatives.

1942

American psychologist Carl Rogers publishes *Counseling and Psychotherapy*, in which he suggests that respect and a nonjudgmental approach to therapy is the foundation for effective treatment of mental health issues.

1990

Ruta Mazelis, who specializes in self-injury disorder, develops and publishes the *Cutting Edge*, a newsletter that is targeted at people who are in any way affected by self-injury.

2000

In a revised edition of the American Psychiatric Association's *Diagnostic and Statistical Manual of Mental Disorders*, the term *self-injury* appears only once—not as a diagnosis, but as a symptom of borderline personality disorder.

2007

After completing a study on self-injurious behavior, researchers from Harvard University and Boston University School of Medicine announce that the strongest factors in whether young people self-injure are sexual abuse and emotional neglect during childhood.

1995

In a BBC television interview, Britain's princess Diana discusses her private struggle in coping with severe emotional pain and reveals that she intentionally cuts her legs and arms.

1990

2000

2010

1991

Psychologist Marsha Linehan publishes a paper about dialectical behavior therapy, a type of treatment that she developed for patients with borderline personality disorder and/or those who self-injure.

2006

Janis Whitlock and colleagues from the Cornell Research Program on Self-Injurious Behavior publish a study titled "Self-Injurious Behavior in a College Population," which shows that one out of five college students have deliberately injured themselves at some point in their lives.

1999

The first Self-Injury Awareness Day is held on March 1; people throughout the United States and other countries widely distribute self-injury fact sheets, reports, and brochures to help increase awareness of self-injurious behavior.

2009

The National Institute of Mental Health launches a study to compare the effectiveness of two treatments, dialectical behavior therapy versus a drug known as fluoxetine, for reducing the risk of self-injury and suicidal behavior in people with borderline personality disorder.

Related Organizations

American Academy of Child and Adolescent Psychiatry (AACAP)

3615 Wisconsin Ave. NW

Washington, DC 20016-3007

phone: (202) 966-7300 • fax: (202) 966-2891

Web site: www.aacap.org

The AACAP is dedicated to treating and improving the quality of life for children and adolescents who suffer from mental, behavioral, or developmental disorders. Its Web site features a number of informative articles and a special "For Families" section that links to a variety of publications.

American Self-Harm Information Clearinghouse (ASHIC)

521 Temple Pl.

Seattle, WA 98122

phone: (206) 604-8963

e-mail: ashic@selfinjury.org • Web site: www.selfinjury.org

The ASHIC strives to educate the general public, as well as health-care professionals, about self-harm. Its Web site offers various articles about self-injury, including fact sheets, common myths, and self-help strategies.

Cornell Research Program on Self-Injurious Behavior (CRPSIB)

Family Life Development Center

Beebe Hall

Cornell University

Ithaca, NY 14853

phone: (607) 255-1861

e-mail: crpsib@cornell.edu • Web site: www.crpsib.com

The CRPSIB conducts research on self-injurious behavior and furnishes its research findings to anyone who is affected by self-injury. An excel-

Related Organizations

lent collection of resources may be found on its Web site, including an "About Self-Injury" section, fact sheets, a discussion forum, and a suggested reading list.

Mayo Clinic

200 First St. SW

Rochester, MN 55905

phone: (507) 284-2511 • fax: (507) 284-0161

Web site: www.mayoclinic.com

The Mayo Clinic is a world-renowned medical facility that is dedicated to patient care, education, and research. A special section of its Web site is dedicated to self-injury disorder and addresses such factors as symptoms, causes, forms of self-injury, risk factors, and complications. A search engine produces a number of articles on related disorders.

Mental Health America

2000 N. Beauregard St., 6th Floor

Alexandria, VA 22311

phone: (703) 684-7722; toll-free: (800) 969-6642

fax: (703) 684-5968

Web site: www.nmha.org

Mental Health America is dedicated to helping all people live mentally healthier lives. A search engine on its Web site produces a collection of publications related to self-injury, including "Fast Facts" and articles about warning signs, treatment options, and support groups.

National Alliance on Mental Illness (NAMI)

3803 N. Fairfax Dr., Suite 100

Arlington, VA 22203

phone: (703) 524-7600 • fax: (703) 524-9094

Web site: www.nami.org

The NAMI is dedicated to improving the lives of individuals and families affected by mental illness. Its Web site features newsletters, press releases, and a search engine that produces a wide variety of articles.

National Institute of Mental Health (NIMH)

Science Writing, Press, and Dissemination Branch

6001 Executive Blvd., Room 8184, MSC 9663

Bethesda, MD 20892-9663

phone: (301) 443-4513; toll-free: (866) 615-6464

fax: (301) 443-4279

e-mail: nimhinfo@nih.gov • Web site: www.nimh.nih.gov

The NIMH seeks to reduce mental illness and behavioral disorders through research and supports science that will improve the diagnosis, treatment, and prevention of mental disorders. Its Web site features statistics, archived *Science News* articles, and a search engine that produces numerous publications about self-injury.

Self Abuse Finally Ends (S.A.F.E.) Alternatives

10 Bergman Ct.

Forest Park, IL 60130

phone: (800) 366-8288 • fax: (888) 296-7988

e-mail: info@selfinjury.com • Web site: www.selfinjury.com

S.A.F.E. Alternatives is a nationally recognized treatment program, professional network, and educational resource base that is committed to helping people overcome self-injurious behavior. Its Web site offers an expansive collection of publications about self-injury, including news articles, frequently asked questions, treatment programs, and a link to the S.A.F.E. blog.

Self Injury Foundation

PO Box 962

South Haven, MI

phone: (888) 962-6774 • fax: (888) 296-7988

e-mail: info@selfinjuryfoundation.org

Web site: www.selfinjuryfoundation.org

The Self Injury Foundation provides research funding, advocacy, support, and education for those who self-injure as well as their families and the professionals who work with them. Its Web site features an "About Self-Injury" section, news articles, a recommended reading list, and a "Q & A" for self injurers, parents, and friends.

To Write Love on Her Arms (TWLOHA)

PO Box 206

Cocoa, FL 32923

phone: (321) 735-0228 • fax: (321) 433-3185

e-mail: info@twloha.com • Web site: www.twloha.com

TWLOHA is a nonprofit movement that is dedicated to presenting hope and finding help for those struggling with depression, addiction, self-injury, and suicide. Its Web site offers news articles, inspirational messages, "Facts" and "Find Help" sections, a list of recommended books, and a link to a blog.

For Further Research

Books

Jerusha Clark, *Inside a Cutter's Mind: Understanding and Helping Those Who Self-Injure*. Colorado Springs, CO: NavPress, 2007.

Gina Giarratano, *On the Cutting Edge: My Struggle with Self-Injury and Mental Illness*. Frederick, MD: PublishAmerica, 2009.

Robert Goolrick, *The End of the World as We Know It: Scenes from a Life*. Chapel Hill, NC: Algonquin, 2007.

Kim Gratz and Alexander Chapman, *Freedom from Self-Harm*. Oakland, CA: New Harbinger, 2009.

Jan Kern, *Scars That Wound, Scars That Heal: A Journey Out of Self-Injury*. Cincinnati: Standard, 2007.

Lori G. Plante, *Bleeding to Ease the Pain*. Westport, CT: Praeger, 2007.

Lawrence E. Shapiro, *Stopping the Pain: A Workbook for Teens Who Cut and Self-Injure*. Oakland, CA: Instant Help, 2008.

Vanessa Vega, *Comes the Darkness, Comes the Light: A Memoir of Cutting, Healing, and Hope*. New York: AMACOM, 2007.

Periodicals

Jessica Bennett, "Why She Cuts," *Newsweek*, December 29, 2008.

Jane E. Brody, "The Growing Wave of Teen Self-Injury," *New York Times*, May 6, 2008.

Johanna Crosby, "A Journey from Self-Abuse to Self-Love," *Cape Cod (MA) Times*, May 29, 2008.

Tracy L. Cross, "Social/Emotional Needs," *Gifted Child Today*, Summer 2007.

Kathiann M. Kowalski, "The Unkindest Cut," *Current Health 2*, a *Weekly Reader* publication, January 2008.

Julie Liotine, "Not Just Skin Deep," *Chicago Parent*, May 25, 2007.

Tara Prutsman, "My Shameful Secret," *Cosmopolitan*, February 2008.

Shari Roan, "Self-Injury on the Rise Among Young People," *Los Angeles Times*, December 8, 2008.

Katie S., "Self-Harm: Can Someone Please Help?" *Indian Life*, January/February 2007.

Internet Sources

Tracy Alderman, "The Scarred Soul," *Psychology Today* blog, October 7, 2009. www.psychologytoday.com/blog/the-scarred-soul/200910/self-injury-myths-and-misconceptions-part-1.

Brittany Burden, "From Self-Injury to Safety," *Oklahoma Daily*, February 25, 2009. http://oudaily.com/news/2009/feb/25/self-injury-safety.

Charlene Laino, "Severe Self-Injury a Threat to Teens," WebMD, December 3, 2008. www.webmd.com/mental-health/news/20081202/severe-self-injury-a-threat-to-teens.

Deb Martinson, "Self-Injury: Fact Sheet (Beyond the Myths)," eNotAlone, 2009. www.enotalone.com/article/2996.html.

Mayo Clinic, "Self-Injury/Cutting," August 2, 2008. www.mayoclinic.com/health/self-injury/DS00775.

Susan Pedersen, "The Dark World of Self-Injury," *Avenue*, August 28, 2009. www.avenuecalgary.com/articles/page/item/the-dark-world-of-self-injury.

Lawrence Rubin and Michael Brody, "Popular Culture Meets Society," *Psychology Today* blog, July 2, 2009. www.psychologytoday.com/blog/popular-culture-meets-psychology/200907/tattoos-and-body-piercing-adolescent-self-expression-or.

Kristalyn Salters-Pedneault, "Self Mutilation," About.com, July 25, 2008. http://bpd.about.com/od/understandingbpd/a/selfharm.htm.

Thomas C. Weiss, "Self Injury Awareness Information," *Disabled World*, January 31, 2009. www.disabled-world.com/disability/awareness/self-injury-awareness.php.

Source Notes

Overview

1. Quoted in Jessica Bennett, "Why She Cuts," *Newsweek*, December 29, 2008. www.newsweek.com.
2. Quoted in Bennett, "Why She Cuts."
3. Quoted in Bennett, "Why She Cuts."
4. Quoted in Michael Hollander, *Helping Teens Who Cut*. New York: Guilford, 2008, p. 3.
5. Deb Martinson, "Self-Injury: Fact Sheet (Beyond the Myths)," eNotAlone, 2009. www.enotalone.com.
6. Vanessa Vega, *Comes the Darkness, Comes the Light: A Memoir of Cutting, Healing, and Hope*. New York: AMACOM, 2007, p. ix.
7. Mayo Clinic, "Self-Injury/Cutting," August 2, 2008. www.mayoclinic.com.
8. Quoted in Lynn K. Jones, "Bleeding to Stop the Hurt: The Rise of Self-Injury," *Social Work Today*, June 16, 2009. www.selfinjury.com.
9. Quoted in Jones, "Bleeding to Stop the Hurt."
10. Hollander, *Helping Teens Who Cut*, p. 18.
11. Mayo Clinic, "Self-Injury/Cutting."
12. Sharon Farber, interviewed by David Roberts, "Getting Help for Self-Harm," HealthyPlace, April 11, 2007. www.healthyplace.com.
13. Lauren Simmons (pseudonym), interview with author, January 5, 2008.
14. Harold Doherty, "Why I Find No Joy in Autism—Biting and Other Self-Injurious Behavior," Facing Autism in New Brunswick blog, January 16, 2008. http://autisminnb.blogspot.com.
15. Mayo Clinic, "Self-Injury/Cutting."
16. Tara Prutsman, "My Shameful Secret," *Cosmopolitan*, February 2008, p. 148.
17. Prutsman, "My Shameful Secret, p. 148."

What Is Self-Injury Disorder?

18. Hollander, *Helping Teens Who Cut*, p. vii.
19. Hollander, *Helping Teens Who Cut*, p. 7.
20. Martinson, "Self-Injury."
21. Quoted in Johanna Crosby, "A Journey from Self-Abuse to Self-Love," *Cape Cod (MA) Times*, May 29, 2008. www.capecodonline.com.
22. Farber, interviewed by Roberts, "Getting Help for Self-Harm."
23. Brittany Burden, "From Self-Injury to Safety," *Oklahoma Daily*, February 25, 2009. http://oudaily.com.
24. Burden, "From Self-Injury to Safety."
25. Hollander, *Helping Teens Who Cut*, p. 67.
26. Vega, *Comes the Darkness, Comes the Light*, p. 3.
27. Vega, *Comes the Darkness, Comes the Light*, p. 1.
28. Vega, *Comes the Darkness, Comes the Light*, pp. 3–4.
29. Quoted in Bennett, "Why She Cuts."
30. Quoted in Bennett, "Why She Cuts."
31. Farber, interviewed by Roberts, "Getting Help for Self-Harm."
32. Quoted in Tracy Swartz, "Hooked on Suspension," *Chicago Tribune Redeye*, November 9, 2007. www.selfinjury.com.
33. Quoted in Hollander, *Helping Teens Who Cut*, p. 14.

Why Do People Intentionally Injure Themselves?

34. Quoted in Hollander, *Helping Teens Who Cut*, p. 13.

35. Quoted in Bennett, "Why She Cuts."
36. Martinson, "Self-Injury."
37. Farber, interviewed by Roberts, "Getting Help for Self-Harm."
38. Martinson, "Self-Injury."
39. Prutsman, "My Shameful Secret."
40. Prutsman, "My Shameful Secret."
41. Lisa H. Glassman, Mariann R. Weierich, Jill M. Hooley, Tata L. Deliberto, and Matthew K. Nock, "Child Maltreatment, Non-suicidal Self-Injury, and the Mediating Role of Self-Criticism," *Behavior Research and Therapy*, April 11, 2007. www.wjh. harvard.edu.
42. Wendy Lader, interviewed by David Roberts, "Treatment for Self-Injury," HealthyPlace, April 11, 2007. www. healthyplace.com.
43. Martinson, "Self-Injury."
44. Sheila E. Crowell et al., "Parent-Child Interactions, Peripheral Serotonin, and Self-Inflicted Injury in Adolescents," *Journal of Consulting and Clinical Psychology*, no. 1, 2008. http:// tbeauchaine.psych.washington.edu.
45. National Institute of Mental Health, "Borderline Personality Disorder," May 13, 2009. www.nimh.nih.gov.
46. HealthyPlace, "An Overview of Depression," January 6, 2009. www. healthyplace.com.
47. Hollander, *Helping Teens Who Cut*, p. 68.

What Are the Prevention and Treatment Options for Self-Injurers?

48. Sandra Shapiro, "Addressing Self-Injury in the School Setting," *Journal of School Nursing*, 2008. http://jsn. sagepub.com.
49. Barent Walsh, interviewed by David Van Nuys, "An Interview with Barent Walsh, Ph.D. on the Nature and Treatment of Self-Injury," Mental-Help, March 30, 2009. www.mental help.net.
50. Michelle Seliner, interviewed by Natalie, "Treating Self-Injury," Healthy-Place, April 11, 2007. www.healthy place.com.
51. Randi Kreger, "Dialectical Behavior Therapy," BPD Central, 2007. www. bpdcentral.com.
52. Quoted in Kreger, "Dialectical Behavior Therapy."
53. Hollander, *Helping Teens Who Cut*, p. 74.
54. Farber, interviewed by Roberts, "Getting Help for Self-Harm."
55. Farber, interviewed by Roberts, "Getting Help for Self-Harm."
56. Meryl Quinn, "A Cutter Offers Insights into Self-Injury," Associated Content, October 25, 2007. www.asso ciatedcontent.com.
57. Quinn, "A Cutter Offers Insights into Self-Injury."
58. Ruta Mazelis, "Living with and Healing from Self-Injury (Self-Inflicted Violence)," Sidran Institute, January 22, 2008. http://download.ncadi.samhsa. gov.
59. Quinn, "A Cutter Offers Insights into Self-Injury."
60. Hollander, *Helping Teens Who Cut*, p. 15.
61. Hollander, *Helping Teens Who Cut*, p. 15.

Can People Overcome Self-Injury Disorder?

62. Quoted in Crosby, "A Journey from Self-Abuse to Self-Love."
63. Quoted in Crosby, "A Journey from Self-Abuse to Self-Love."
64. Quoted in Crosby, "A Journey from Self-Abuse to Self-Love."
65. Burden, "From Self-Injury to Safety."
66. Brittany Burden, "From the Hospital to Home," *Oklahoma Daily*, February 26, 2009. http://oudaily.com.

67. Quoted in Julie Liotine, "Not Just Skin Deep," *Chicago Parent*, May 25, 2007. www.selfinjury.com.

68. Quoted in Crosby, "A Journey from Self-Abuse to Self-Love."

69. Quoted in Molly Page, "'It Became an Addiction,'" *Charleston (WV) Gazette*, March 1, 2008. http://sundaygazette-mail.com.

70. Quoted in Page, "'It Became an Addiction.'"

71. Quoted in Page, "'It Became an Addiction.'"

72. Quoted in Page, "'It Became an Addiction.'"

73. Quoted in Page, "'It Became an Addiction.'"

74. Quoted in Brandy Hadden, "Self-Injury Awareness Grows," *Clarion Call*, November 11, 2009. www.clarioncall news.com.

75. Sylvermoon, "I Can't Fight the Urge," Self-Injury Support Group, October 3, 2009. www.dailystrength.org.

76. Andrew Daniel Evans, "Self-Mutilation: Self-Mutilation Addiction," AllExperts, September 9, 2009. http://en.allexperts. com.

77. Burden, "From the Hospital to Home."

List of Illustrations

What Is Self-Injury Disorder?
Self-Injury and Gender   31
Self-Injurious Behavior Among College Students   32
Why and How People Harm Themselves   33

Why Do People Intentionally Injure Themselves?
Self-Injury Risk Factors   45
The Role of Childhood Abuse   46
Self-Injury as an Addiction   47

What Are the Prevention and Treatment Options for Self-Injurers?
A Successful Prevention Strategy   60
A Successful Treatment Strategy   61
A Residential Program Shows Results   62

Can People Overcome Self-Injury Disorder?
Substitutes for Self-Injury   74
Most Self-Injurers Do Not Seek Help   75
Self-Harm and the Internet   76

Index

abuse
  childhood, percent of self-
    injurers reporting, 46 (chart)
  as factor in self-injury, 44
addiction, self-injury disorder as,
  47 (chart), 56, 68
adolescents
  prevalence of self-injury among,
    15, 30
  suicide as cause of death among,
    48
adults, self-injury among, 14
Aleksovski, Goce, 42
American Journal of Psychiatry, 77
American Psychological
  Association, 35
American Self-Harm Information
  Clearinghouse (ASHIC), 67
anti-anxiety medications, 73
antidepressants, 73
attention seeking, is not motive
  for self-injury, 10, 53–54
auditory hallucinations, 22–24
autism
  likelihood of self-injury in
    children with, 44
  self-injury disorder and, 16–17

Bagnato, Becki, 8–9
Baugh, Michael, 51
behavior therapy. *See* dialectical
  behavior therapy
borderline personality disorder
  (BPD), 7, 35
  effectiveness of dialectical
    behavior therapy in, 62
  self-injury in, 38–39
BPD. *See* borderline personality

disorder
Burden, Brittany, 8, 22, 34,
  64–65, 69

Caicedo, Saskya, 41
*Canadian Medical Association
  Journal,* 30
Centers for Disease Control and
  Prevention (CDC), 61
Chakraburtty, Amal, 29, 70
Charleston (WV) *Gazette*
  (newspaper), 66
Child Health Literature Review
  (newsletter), 77
Comprehensive Psychiatry (journal),
  44
Conterio, Karen, 76
Croft, Harry, 48
Cross, Tracy L., 28
Crowell, Sheila E., 27
Cutter, Deborah, 29, 56
cutting, 10, 13 (illustration)
  as most common self-injury, 6

depression, 7
  causes of, 39
  failure to seek treatment for, 73
diagnosis, 15, 17–18
*Diagnostic and Statistical Manual
  of Mental Disorders* (DSM), 35
dialectical behavior therapy
  (DBT), 50–52
  effectiveness of, 74, 77
  frequency of self-injury before/
    after, 61 (chart)
    in residential treatment, 62
    (chart)
distress tolerance, 51

Index

Doherty, Harold, 16–17

eating disorder
  association with self-injury and,
    16
  prevalence of self-injury in adult
    women with, 44
Eliminate the Stigma of Mental
  Illness (blog), 10
embedding, 25
emergency room visits, numbers
  due to intentional injuries, 61
emotional pain
  as most common factor in self-
    injury, 6
  self-injury helps offset, 9–10, 20
endorphins, 46, 47
Evans, Andrew Daniel, 68
exercise, 77

Farber, Sharon, 16, 22, 42, 72
  on childhood trauma, 35–36
  on giving up self-injurious
    behavior, 52
  on passive self-injury, 25
  on suicide among self-injurers,
    28

gender, self-injury and, 14, 31
  (chart)
Goolrick, Robert, 71

Hanagan, Connie, 21, 63–64, 65
Hatz, Jennifer, 10
Healthy Place (Web site), 39, 42
Hollander, Michael, 9–10, 12,
  14–15, 20–21, 27, 57
  on auditory hallucinations,
    22–23
  on cause of self-harming
    behavior, 42
  on dialectical behavior therapy,
    51–52, 74
  on OCD and self-injury, 40
  on self-injurious behavior as
    attention-seeking, 54
hospitalization, forced, 53

Internet discussion groups,
  effectiveness of, 59, 76 (chart)
interpersonal effectiveness, 51

Journal of Clinical Psychology, 74
*Journal of Consulting and Clinical
  Psychology*, 14, 30, 38
*Journal of Mental Health
  Counseling*, 76
Journal of School Nursing, 48
Journal of Youth and Adolescence,
  50, 59

King, Steven A., 34
Kreger, Randi, 50–51

Lader, Wendy, 12, 25, 37–38, 76
Laumann, Anne, 25–26
Lepore, Mark, 67
LifeSIGNS, 20, 57
Linehan, Marsha, 50

Martinson, Deb, 21, 43, 67
  on inappropriate treatment of
    self-injurers, 57
  on self-injury and emotional
    pain, 35, 36
  on serotonin and self-injury, 38
  on suicide and self-injury, 10
Mayo Clinic, 12, 28
  on family history of self-
    injurious behavior, 45
  on guilt associated with self-
    injury disorder, 8
  on prevention of self-injury
    disorders, 18

on reasons for self-injury, 15
on role of family history of self-
destructive acts, 37
on treatment of self-injury
disorder, 48
Mazelis, Ruta, 29, 53, 58, 71

Nagy, Donna, 65
National Institutes of Mental
Health (NIMH), 38, 62
National Self-Injury Awareness
Day, 67
Newsweek (magazine), 30
nicotine dependence, as factor in
self-injury among girls, 44

obsessive-compulsive disorder
(OCD), 7
self-injury in, 39–40
OCD. *See* obsessive-compulsive
disorder

prevention/prevention programs,
7, 48–49, 59
strategy for, 60 (chart)
Prutsman, Tara, 18–19, 36–37
Psychiatry (journal), 44, 59

Quinn, Meryl, 52—53, 54, 63

S.A.F.E. (Self Abuse Finally Ends)
Alternatives program, 18, 50,
65, 72, 75
strategy of, 58
success rate of, 73
SANE, 30
Screening for Mental Health, 49
self-inflicted injuries
emergency room visits due to,
61
methods of, 6, 33 (chart)
reasons given for, 9, 33 (chart)

types of, 10–12
self-injurers
come from all walks of life, 12,
14
effectiveness of substitutes for
injury for, 74 (chart)
likelihood of attempting suicide
among, 7, 12
prevalence of childhood abuse
among, 46 (chart)
rates of help-seeking among, 75
(chart)
should not be forcibly stopped
from injuring, 52–53
some cannot recover, 68
self-injury disorder
as addiction, 47 (chart), 56, 68
awareness/education efforts for,
67–68
complications of, 6, 12
definition of, 6
diagnosis of, 15, 17–18
is not about attention-seeking,
53–54
prevalence of, 14
among college students, 31,
32 (chart)
gender differences in, 30, 31
(chart)
risk factors for, 7, 37, 45, 45
(table)
Seliner, Michelle, 14, 50, 56, 63,
68
Serani, Deborah, 70
serotonin, 43
self-injurious behavior and
imbalance in, 38, 39, 45
Shapiro, Sandra, 48–49
Shiels, William, 24, 44
Signs of Self-Injury program,
49–50
Simmons, Lauren, 16

substance abuse, risk for self-injurers who stop injuring without therapy, 75
substitutes for self-injury, effectiveness of, 74 (chart)
suicide, 28
    likelihood of self-injurers to attempt, 7, 12
    most self-injurers do not intend, 10
    percent of teen self-injurers attempting, 59
    prevalence of, 7
    risk of, 7
surveys
    on prevalence of self-injury among college students, 14, 31
    among high school students, 30
    of self-injurers
        adolescent, on reasons/methods for self-injury, 33 (chart)
        on being abused as children, 46 (chart)
        on helpfulness of having support available, 76
        on helpfulness of Internet

support groups, 76
suspension, 24, 25–26

Thompson, Colleen, 20, 43, 72
Thompson, Travis, 17
treatment, 7
    with antidepressants/anti-anxiety drugs, 18, 73
    many self-injurers do not seek, 59
    success of among adolescents, 74
    See also dialectical behavior therapy
Truth Hurts, 30
Tsokatos, Amourena, 25

van der Kolk, Bessel, 35
Vega, Vanessa, 11, 23–24, 41, 57, 71

Walsh, Barent, 49
Wardell, Scott, 43
WebMD (Web site), 43
Weissman, Myrna M., 28
Whitlock, Janis, 14, 41, 76
women, self-injury and eating disorders among, 44

About the Author

Peggy J. Parks holds a bachelor of science degree from Aquinas College in Grand Rapids, Michigan, where she graduated magna cum laude. She has written more than 90 nonfiction educational books for children and young adults, as well as self-published a cookbook called *Welcome Home: Recipes, Memories, and Traditions from the Heart.* Parks lives in Muskegon, Michigan, a town that she says inspires her writing because of its location on the shores of Lake Michigan.